Praise for *The Gentle Art of Discipling Women*

If you've ever felt intimidated when a young woman asks if you will disciple her, read this book! In *The Gentle Art of Discipling Women,* Dana Yeakley has included everything you need to know when you say yes to the exciting opportunity of investing in the life of someone who wants to grow in her faith. You will learn how to be a disciple and how to take specific action steps to make disciples. This is a must-have resource!

CAROL KENT
Speaker and author of *Becoming a Woman of Influence*

Dana Yeakley's passion for discipleship is both inspiring and infectious. In her book *The Gentle Art of Discipling Women,* Dana provides a guide that removes the mystery from discipleship. Grounded in Scripture and supported by personal stories, this book will make you feel both encouraged and empowered to live out the command for every believer to "go and make disciples."

JENNI CATRON
Church leader and author of *The 4 Dimensions of Extraordinary Leadership*

Through the pages of this book, experienced discipler Dana Yeakley comes alongside those of us who want to disciple women but aren't sure how to start, whom to approach, what to do, or how to keep things on track to show us the way. This book is a great resource for any woman who wants a front row seat to see the Word of God bring change to the life of another woman.

NANCY GUTHRIE
Bible teacher and author of the *Seeing Jesus in the Old Testament* Bible study series

In a culture where our identity is often focused on what we do, Dana places equal emphasis on being a mature disciple before we do anything for God. With a solid foundation of faith and security in our identity in Christ, we can confidently engage others with proper motivation and intentionally colabor with God in the gentle art of disciplemaking.

KIMBERLY MATTHISEN
Alongside Women and National Leadership Team, Navigators of Canada

Dana's book is full of important, life-giving lessons on both being a disciple and leading others in purposeful discipleship relationships. A great tool for every woman who takes Jesus' call to "go and make disciples" seriously.

JESSIE MINASSIAN
Resident "big sis" at LifeLoveandGod.com and author of *Unashamed*

THE GENTLE

art of discipling women

THE GENTLE

ART OF

discipling

WOMEN

NURTURING AUTHENTIC FAITH
IN OURSELVES AND OTHERS

DANA YEAKLEY

A NavPress resource published in alliance
with Tyndale House Publishers, Inc.

NAVPRESS⬤®

NavPress is the publishing ministry of The Navigators, an international Christian organization and leader in personal spiritual development. NavPress is committed to helping people grow spiritually and enjoy lives of meaning and hope through personal and group resources that are biblically rooted, culturally relevant, and highly practical.

For more information, visit www.NavPress.com.

Library of Congress Cataloging-in-Publication Data
Yeakley, Dana.
 The gentle art of discipling women : nurturing authentic faith in ourselves and others / Dana Yeakley.
  pages cm
 Includes bibliographical references.
 ISBN 978-1-63146-382-2
 1. Church work with women. 2. Discipling (Christianity) I. Title.
 BV4445.Y43 2016
 259.082--dc23   2015033532

Printed in the United States of America

21	20	19	18	17	16	15
7	6	5	4	3	2	1

To my mom and her mom, Mammaw, who modeled a life of faith and prayer and passed their love for Jesus on to me.

Contents

Introduction *XI*

PART ONE: *Be His Disciple* 1

CHAPTER ONE: *We Are Forgiven* 5

CHAPTER TWO: *We Are Safe* 19

CHAPTER THREE: *We Have Access* 33

CHAPTER FOUR: *We Are Becoming* 49

PART TWO: *Make a Disciple* 69

CHAPTER FIVE: *How Do We Create a Life-Giving Atmosphere?* 77

CHAPTER SIX: *Whom Do We Help?* 101

CHAPTER SEVEN: *What Do We Share?* 119

CHAPTER EIGHT: *How Does Discipling One-on-One Actually Work?* 149

Leader's Guide *173*

Notes *179*

Introduction

DESIGNED FOR DISCIPLESHIP

Emily fidgeted with her coffee cup. Marcia was running late. They'd gotten to know each other a little at church. Emily, though honored, had been taken aback when Marcia, a new Christian, had asked Emily to disciple her. She had stammered out a yes without thinking and now was wondering what exactly she'd gotten herself into. Emily was a Christian—had been following Jesus for years—and of course she knew she was *supposed* to be discipling people. Something within her longed to help Marcia grow. But now, in the midst of this busy coffee shop, her coffee going cold and her mind going blank, she felt utterly inadequate. Marcia was looking for her to do something, but Emily had no idea where to start.

Have you ever felt this way? Maybe you haven't thought of it in terms of the word *discipleship*, but perhaps someone has asked you to help her grow, or simply has looked to you for guidance in her relationship with Christ—and you feel ill-equipped to do whatever this "discipling" thing is supposed to be.

What do you think when you hear the word *discipleship*? A lot of us might look at Jesus' command in Matthew 28 to "go and make disciples of all nations," and we nod our heads. But when we get down to it, the actual "going and making disciples" part can feel intimidating, insurmountable, or simply confusing.

Even though we want to—and in fact are designed—to disciple others, we let our confusion and lack of information hold us hostage. Later in this book we will get to Jesus' definition of *discipleship*—our most important guide for discipling—but to get started, let's consider the dictionary definition Daniel Webster gives us: "Someone who accepts and helps to spread the teachings of a famous person."[1] Webster nails it! Indeed, discipleship means accepting and helping to spread the words of Jesus. Could it really be that simple?

Yes, discipling another woman is a doable task. Throughout this book, I want to walk alongside you, encouraging you to find your God-given ability to disciple another woman in your life. I'll be with you in spirit as you uncover the assurance and freedom God offers each of His daughters who want to follow Him in obedience into this gentle art of discipling women.

WHY "GENTLE"?

> The LORD and King is coming with power.
>> He rules with a powerful arm.
> He has set his people free.
>> He is bringing them back as his reward.
>> He has won the battle over their enemies.
> He takes care of his flock like a shepherd.
>> He gathers the lambs in his arms.
> He carries them close to his heart.
>> He gently leads those that have little ones.
>
> ISAIAH 40:10-11

Isaiah 40:10 shows us a bold and compelling description of our almighty God—and in the very next verse, this same God is described as a protective shepherd who gently gathers lambs in His arms. If we wish to disciple other women, we need that powerful ruler supernaturally surrounding us and filling us—but we can also be thankful knowing that He attends us and those we help as a gentle shepherd. We can gently disciple others with His omnipotent pastoral care and support.

As our gentle shepherd, Jesus "gently leads those that have little ones" (v. 11). When I read this, I picture a young mother holding her newborn. There is never a more vulnerable time for mother or baby than the first days or weeks of the little one's life! I remember the vulnerability I felt as I raised my three children, and more recently I have watched the empathetic care of my daughters for their children. As women, we have been created with that sensitivity and vulnerability whether we have had children or not.

Biologically, there are hormones every woman needs: estrogen, oxytocin, and progesterone. Sometimes I refer to these hormones as "drugs" that we have been placed on so that we can do what we are created to do! We have all experienced the side effects of these "drugs" when we experience PMS, but these hormones also give us wonderful capabilities. We are able to sense what people—whether our friends, husbands, or children—need. We can quickly tell how someone else feels. Sometimes it seems as though we have eyes in the back of our heads!

This nurturing quality we possess within our feminine design is our greatest resource as we respond to Christ's call to make disciples. Disciplers are nourishers. They are sensitive. They are relationally aware. They give attention to the spiritual dietary needs of those they help. They place themselves in a position of vulnerability for the sake of those they help. And because Jesus gently cares for us and leads us, we are compelled to gently disciple others.

I am thankful for the gentleness that Jesus has continued to show me throughout my life as I have walked with Him. And how important it is that we offer gentleness as we disciple! This gentleness does not mean that we are indifferent to the damaging life choices or attitudes of those around us. Nor does it mean that we endorse the pervasive victim mentalities present in our culture today that paralyze a woman's growth. But in gentleness, we should show deliberate voluntary kindness and forbearance as we conduct ourselves as disciplers.

WHY AN "ART"?

Like art, discipling requires a certain level of skill development. The application of those skills, along with creative acumen, brings discipling to a level of artistry. As artists, we envision the beautiful results of what is being crafted, plan for the results, and contribute to their end. We are fully present with the emerging work of beauty in front of us, even as we work with the finished product constantly in mind. Being flexible and creative as we use the skills we have developed is essential as we trust God for His desired outcome in a woman's life.

As we intentionally develop our skills, we grow in our ability to disciple with confident thoroughness. Relying upon God's Spirit helps us cultivate an awareness of the needs of those we help. And while we are "at work" in a person's life, the ultimate Artist, the Creator of the universe, is accomplishing the true work! God is far more in tune and active with those we are discipling than we could ever hope to be.

> LORD, you have seen what is in my heart.
>   You know all about me.
> You know when I sit down and when I get up.
>   You know what I'm thinking even though
>   you are far away.

You know when I go out to work
    and when I come back home.
You know exactly how I live.
LORD, even before I speak a word,
    you know all about it.

You are all around me, behind me and in front of me.
    You hold me safe in your hand.
I'm amazed at how well you know me.
    It's more than I can understand.

PSALM 139:1-6

HOW TO USE THIS BOOK

Today, if we want to grow in Christ, women have so many options! The Sunday morning worship service, Sunday school for adults, Tuesday or Wednesday morning or evening Bible study, the Christmas evangelistic brunch, perhaps a fall or spring retreat, conferences . . . the list goes on.

In my twenties and thirties, I was always involved in women's groups at church. I loved the camaraderie these communities provided as I began raising kids, hunkering down in the marriage relationship, and figuring out what it meant to be a godly woman. The friends I made during these years were priceless and necessary.

But during those years I was especially helped in my growth through a one-on-one discipleship relationship with a woman ten years older than me. She helped me in my personal walk with God, in my understanding of the Word, and in my conviction that I needed to help others know Christ and make Him known. This one-on-one discipleship attention influenced my life choices and helped me make sense of all the other input I was receiving from the pulpit, conference speakers, and Christian friends in Bible study and other groups I attended.

The Gentle Art of Discipling Women was written to help women who want to disciple another woman one-on-one. Remember Emily at the beginning of this chapter? If you're like Emily, desiring to disciple someone but unsure where to begin, I would recommend that you go through this book on your own, asking yourself, "Am I grounded in Christ?" and "How do I disciple someone else?" This book will equip the mature Christian who wants to disciple another—but it will also be of help to the woman who wishes to be discipled! If you're like Marcia, desiring to be discipled, you could pick up this book and ask a trusted and respected fellow believer, "Could we read this book together? Can you help me grow as we do so?"

This book can also be used with a small group. Perhaps you have several friends who are full of life and would be great at discipling others. Take a risk and invite them to study this book together. There is a short leader's guide in the back of this book that will give you guidance and confidence to guide others along this journey with you. Walking together through both sections of this book will give all of you a chance to talk about your strengths and weaknesses as His disciple and to encourage one another as you step out to disciple others. Understanding that we are all in this together is important as we think through the possibilities of discipling! Be encouraged by Psalm 68:11: "The Lord announces the word, and the women who proclaim it are a mighty throng" (NIV). Come join the mighty throng and take up the challenge of discipling others!

Do you remember our simple dictionary definition of *discipleship*? Discipleship means accepting and helping to spread the words of Jesus. Both pieces are critical as we step into discipling another woman. So this book is divided into two parts: "Be His Disciple" and "Make a Disciple."

Part 1 is vital: *being* one who authentically follows Christ must always precede stepping out and building into someone else's life. So, in this first section, we will forthrightly consider our own foundation—what we as Jesus' disciples need for our own spiritual health as we walk with Him. These things are our birthright as His daughters!

Take your time to work through the stories, Scripture, and questions in this section. Studying Scripture is a crucial part of both your individual walk with Christ and your journey alongside someone else. Throughout this book, we will dive into Scripture to help us understand key truths about our position in Christ as a disciple and how we are to disciple others. Use a journal to reflect on the questions about Scripture and record your thoughts. The questions are designed to be worked through as you go through each chapter, and you may wish to take a week to go through each chapter to adequately dig into the questions. This part of the book is intended to help you personally, and it can also serve as a powerful study tool with which you can disciple another woman in her understanding of who she is in Christ. I pray that God uses it mightily in your own faith so you may be confident as you set out to disciple others.

Part 2 calls us to boldly consider and step into the broad scope of what it means to be a disciplemaker. We will look at Jesus as our master disciplemaker. We will consider advice on making disciples as we look at the Word as our backdrop. As we work through the Scripture, questions, and challenges together, you will feel empowered and encouraged, understanding that God has given you all you need to disciple others!

God's heart is that we would join Him in the lofty mission of bringing others to Himself and discipling them so that they might go and do the same. As we consider joining Christ's commission upon our lives, let us humbly lean upon Him because He promises to be with us and gently lead us. Step with me into the magnificent challenge of impacting our world through investing in another person![2]

❦ PART ONE ❦

Be His Disciple

I DON'T CARE who tries to convince us that there are simple for-mulas for a happy life—life is not easy. If someone says that knowing Christ means painless living, then they are passing on an enormous lie. But do you know what Jesus does prom-ise us? "I have come so they may have life. I want them to have it in the fullest possible way" (John 10:10).

The word Jesus used for *life* in this verse is translated from the Greek word *zoe*:

> *Zoe* is distinguished from *bios* (*Strong's*, 979) which
> refers to physical life or livelihood. Having *bios*
> allows us to be physically alive, that is to exist.
> *Zoe* (*Strong's*, 2222) is the nobler word of the two,
> expressing all of the highest and best which Christ is
> and which He gives to the saints. *Zoe* is the highest
> blessedness of the creature.[3]

We all possess *bios*, but some of us may not be experiencing or living out of the wealth of *zoe*, the life that Christ gives us. Jesus' purpose in coming to earth was not only to die for our sins but to open the way to a life that is full and meaningful. As we examine our foundation of faith in this section, consider: Are we living abundantly, in living color, as Jesus intends—or are we just existing as in a dull black-and-white photo? Are we truly living, or just existing?

FOUNDATION

In these first four chapters, we will spend time digging into four foundational realities of our faith:

- We Are Forgiven
- We Are Safe
- We Have Access
- We Are Becoming

These realities are for every follower of Christ, and incredibly important for those of us who want to take up the gentle art of discipling women. As we consider discipling, we need to be assured of our place as His disciple so we pass on that which we know to be true. These four realities flow from the truth of the Word of God and center on the promises we have in Christ. Living in these realities cultivates an authentic faith that will underscore every part of our lives—and will undergird us as we gently offer help and growth to those we disciple.

We Are Forgiven: Knowing that we are forgiven is crucial to a genuine faith, because without knowing the eternal and daily reality of God's forgiveness, we tend to live out a self-serving vacuous existence even as we call ourselves "Christian." Our lives will not center on Christ and joyful obedience to His Word but will merely give Him a compartment or two, allowing us to pretend we're following Christ. When we truly embrace and hinge all that we do on the sacrificial forgiveness of God, then we begin to acknowledge daily how spiritually destitute we are apart from Him. Having this reality firmly established in our hearts will launch us into an ability to care and lead another as we disciple them.

We Are Safe: Do you know that you are safe in Christ? Only when we embrace this reality can we walk with Him day by day free from anxiety. Our media-driven world can create fear and panic; it is vital to understand that though we are vulnerable, we are shielded in Christ. As we comprehend this, we can live out of His protection. And from there we bring our strength and conviction to the discipling table. Genuine faith rests upon our consciousness that we are safe because of the trustworthiness of our God, who not only created us but has arranged for us an eternal home.

We Have Access: Most of us live inside stressful, active, overwhelming schedules, under the burden of a myriad of expectations. Cultivating intimacy with Christ is imperative. In the protection of our daily connection to Him, we can not only survive but thrive above the cacophony that surrounds us. As we set out to disciple other women, this reality will extend blessing into the lives of those we help.

We Are Becoming: The truth that "we are becoming" impacts how we perceive every circumstance of our lives. Christ makes no mistakes. We are the work in progress of a loving God, and He intends to complete His work in us. The abundant life that Jesus promises involves His personal and loving invasion into our spirits as He matures our character to wholly reflect Himself. As we come alongside another woman, we will have empathy and understanding for her life circumstances and relationships—because we are also in the process of becoming.

The pursuit of a genuine faith requires that we, with vulnerability and honesty, open ourselves to Christ, anticipating growth that takes us out of our comfort zone. And as we engage in this study with other women, we have the opportunity to encourage and challenge one another on the journey.

CHAPTER ONE

We Are Forgiven

Christ [the Messiah Himself] died for sins once for all, the Righteous for the unrighteous (the Just for the unjust, the Innocent for the guilty), that He might bring us to God. ❧ 1 PETER 3:18, AMP

Jesus said to her, "Your sins are forgiven." The other guests began to talk about this among themselves. They said, "Who is this who even forgives sins?" ❧ LUKE 7:48-49

Forgive us our sins, as we also forgive everyone who sins against us. ❧ LUKE 11:4

HAVE YOU EVER DEALT with an addiction? I'm not just talking about the big ones we automatically think of—drugs or alcohol or food, for example—but something, anything, that had such a grip on your life that it colored everything else you did.

I did. In my late twenties and early thirties, I was completely and unabashedly codependent. Unknowingly, I began to rely upon my group of girlfriends to give me my sense of identity. I needed to hear their compliments. I looked forward to and leaned upon their laughter and approval of my ideas, choices, and opinions. Whenever I left an outing or coffee time with them, I felt satisfied. Life was good! It was a satisfying unseen addiction.

And during this time in my life, I was avidly discipling women.

You know, what this book is about.

In the midst of my busy schedule—leading group studies, meeting with women one-on-one, prepping to move overseas as a missionary, raising three children under six years of age, and just really enjoying life—God gently ran interference on my heart. His goal? To intervene in my addiction.

My awareness of this addiction began to bubble up in me when I realized I was finding an unhealthy sense of satisfaction in the fact that a certain really "cool" woman had asked me to disciple her. Meeting with her fed my sense of personal worth. Our discipling relationship was a badge I pompously wore for others to see. As I began to realize the pleasure I was drawing from this "discipling relationship," I was dismayed.

God showed me that this particular situation was but the pinnacle of a great iceberg of codependency. Relying on my cozy group of friends or someone I was discipling for my sense of importance, value, or identity was clearly sin. Not only was this codependency crowding out Jesus as my "first love," but it was becoming an idol that I depended on to give me "life." The full weight of this tendency tormented me deep within my spirit. My heart crumpled as I confessed to Jesus that my identity needs were being met through the very thing He had asked me to do: disciple women.

And, as He always does, He offered me forgiveness with open arms (see 1 John 1:9).

Forgiveness is sometimes difficult for us to understand. Sure, we all know at some level or another that when we come to Christ we are forgiven for all our sin—past, present, and future. But as we live life, we still sin.

And this is the beauty of the gospel: when we first believe in Christ we repent and He makes all things new. But just as exciting is this: that as we continue to sin, Jesus is faithful and just to forgive us our sin! Over and over and over. Choosing to sin, even though we know Christ, and humbly seeking forgiveness are intrinsic aspects of our lifelong trek with Him. So we must continue to walk with Him and let Him transform us completely, continually confessing our sin and receiving His forgiveness. And because He continues to forgive us, we are humbled and glad to forgive others.

As I have developed in my understanding of forgiveness, I have experienced a spiritually tangible God-presence accompanied by His peace. And my love for Him deepens the more I recognize the value and truth of His forgiveness for my sin. Let's explore together this powerful first foundational reality that we are women whom Jesus loves and has forgiven.

AMONG THE FORGIVEN

The Bible is full of stories of people who experienced the power of forgiveness firsthand, but I particularly love the story of the prostitute in Luke 7. As we engage with her life, let's stand beside her, befriend her, and seek to understand her deepest emotions and actions.

As a prostitute, she was socially and culturally condemned for her transgressions. No one could fathom what might have led her into her life of sin. No one in her world cared to understand the shame that she carried with her through a pit of immoral disgrace.

She had sinned. She knew it. And yet she innocently but determinedly moved toward Jesus. She even risked stepping into Simon the Pharisee's judgmental gaze. Without one word she approached, worshiped, and engaged with Jesus. She sought Christ, trusting His forgiveness.

The men in Luke 7 who attended the dinner and observed our forgiven friend found it difficult to wrap their minds around the forgiveness Jesus offered her. Perhaps it was because they knew about her sins, conspicuous and reprehensible. Perhaps she made them feel uncomfortable and a bit nervous as they watched from their pious seats.

Some of my friends have experienced sexual brokenness in one way or another over the course of their lives. It is agonizing to hear of the hurt and shame others inflicted upon them and the resulting poor choices they made as they tried to deal with the pain. Perhaps they have asked, "Could a body broken and blood spilled two thousand years ago restore my own damaged life?"[4]

One such young woman, Janie, grew up making harmful choices because of the sexual wrongdoing committed against her as a child. Hear her heart as she vividly describes the morning when she acknowledged Christ's forgiveness:

> One morning, my friend picked me up for church. I was reluctant to go with her, knowing where I'd been the night before, getting my fill of pleasure and numbing my pain. Nonetheless, I went and listened to what the pastor said. By the end of the service, I was sobbing like someone who had just lost a loved one.
>
> *What is wrong with me? Why am I unraveling?* Before I could think another thought, my feet started moving. *Something* compelled me to walk up to the front of that church. I knelt down with that man and admitted my desperate need to be rescued from my sin-ravaged life. I wish I could describe what happened to my soul at that moment without sounding overly dramatic, but something deeply touched me and changed me on the inside.
>
> For the first time in my life I felt worthy to be loved. I knew I didn't deserve it and I couldn't have earned it, nor could I have made it happen through any effort of my own. The heavy burden I was carrying was being carried by someone else. Someone who took the very stabs to His own soul that I should have received. Someone who bled physical drops of blood to pay the price I owed.

Unfathomable. An indescribable, mysterious
transformation was taking place inside of me.[5]

Janie is a modern-day Luke 7 woman! As she moved
from her sin-ravaged existence into the loving arms of Jesus,
she experienced a kind of spiritual culture shock. Like the
woman of Luke 7, my friend came to the awareness that
Christ loved her—and because of His love she felt worthy to
be loved. Realizing that we matter to Jesus leads us to grasp
what C. S. Lewis points out: "He died not for men, but for
each man. If each man had been the only man made, He
would have done no less."[6] We are uniquely loved and will
be uniquely cared for!

Janie and the woman of Luke 7 remind us that our ultimate source of forgiveness is Jesus Christ. Let's look back
at Him as He connects with our miscreant girlfriend in
Luke 7. Bravely she encountered the living Jesus and worshiped Him, using perfume that she would have formerly
used to allure prospective clients. She physically interacted
with Jesus as she worshiped Him without a word. Her
actions, though passionate, were not seductive. She was
forgiven and free.

Like this forgiven friend in Luke 7, when we fully
embrace the forgiveness of Christ, we receive the agape love
of God. His agape love is deep and constant, extended personally toward those who are entirely unworthy. God's love,
when truly embraced, produces and fosters a reverential
love toward Him and a practical love toward others. And,

ultimately, this love fosters a desire to help others to seek Him. It is this agape love for us that moved God to send His Son, Jesus.

The woman of Luke 7 is every woman. In fact, she is every person! She is you and she is me. She understood that she was forgiven for all of her immoral ways. She saw Jesus for who he was, the Redeeming God. And He received the prostitute's worship and thanksgiving, endorsing the truth of her forgiveness and promising her peace. Because she knew forgiveness for her abundant sin, she wanted to respond to Christ by showing how much she loved Him for forgiving her. She was done with her past way of living.

Of course, Jesus used this woman's life to teach Simon the Pharisee and all who gathered at his table. Where the woman had seen Jesus for who He truly was, Simon the Pharisee saw Jesus as a pathetic slave. He did not welcome Him as an honored guest even though it was required by culture. But what a momentous dinner for those men! Would Simon begin to see Jesus accurately? Would he be able to see Jesus as the forgiving agent that He is? And would Simon ever come to a place in his life where he could offer grace and forgiveness to others?

GO DEEPER

To help us really wrestle with this concept of forgiveness, let's take a closer look at Luke 7. Read verses 36-50 in your favorite translation, then answer the questions in your journal.

Verses 36-37

1. Who was present at this dinner?

2. Why do you think Jesus came to eat dinner with Simon the Pharisee and his friends?

3. The woman brought a flask of perfumed ointment. How did this reflect her purpose in coming to see Jesus?

4. Do you ever plan how you might serve or worship Jesus in a special way that reflects your heart of gratitude?

Verse 38

5. What was her demeanor? Why do you think she acted this way?

6. List all the nonverbal interactions she had with Jesus. How did her actions reflect her past?

7. Through her actions the woman brought honor to Jesus. What insight into the woman's heart does this give you?

Verse 39

8. How did Simon the Pharisee view this woman? What conclusion did Simon make about Jesus because of his view of the woman?

Verses 40-43

9. What was Jesus replying to in these verses? How did He reply?

10. What lesson was Jesus teaching through this parable? How did Simon respond?

11. Jesus spoke to Simon's intellect, not to his emotions. Why do you think He did this?

Verses 44-47

12. Hospitality was highly valued in this culture. Hosts were to bow down to

their guests as they greeted them, kiss them on the cheek, wash their feet, offer them tea, and make them feel incredibly welcome and appreciated. Simon the Pharisee ignored this respectful behavior toward Jesus. What conclusions do you draw about Simon because of this?

13. What is the lesson Jesus is teaching all of us through this woman's life?

14. Why do you think this woman loved much? Do you identify with her deep sense of love for Christ?

15. What was this woman's love rooted in?

16. Read John 14:21. What do you see in this verse about loving Jesus?

Verse 48

17. Jesus had already said that her sins were forgiven. Why do you think He repeated this truth to her?

Verse 49

18. What was it that the guests at the table began to question about forgiveness?

19. Why do you think Jesus wanted these men to know that He forgives sins?

Verse 50

20. What saved this woman?

21. Why do you think Jesus told her to "go in peace"? Do you think peace is a benefit of experiencing forgiveness? Why or why not?

THE REALITY OF FORGIVENESS

We are forgiven! Easy to breeze past this foundational reality, isn't it? But without a transformative realization of what Jesus has truly done for us, we may feel hindered as we step forward in making disciples. We can't be effective disciple-makers if we choose to live under a dark undefined label that

13

says we are *unforgiven* when in truth Jesus calls us *forgiven and free*! This is an opportune time for you to settle from the heart those things that weigh you down or hold you back from a spiritual fresh start.

As we pursue this essential and foundational reality of forgiveness, we must also contemplate our willingness to forgive others (see Luke 11:4). Because of what Christ has done for us we can compassionately move toward those who have hurt us deeply, slandered us, lied about us, talked behind our backs, wounded us deeply through physically abusive acts, or passed over us for compensation or honor. C. S. Lewis reminds us, "To be a Christian means to forgive the inexcusable because God has forgiven the inexcusable in you."[7]

Forgiving those who have deeply hurt us definitely takes work. We cannot simply flippantly say, "It's okay." My friend Terri, who had forgiven the uncle who abused her at age six, told me that "twenty years later, after I had forgiven my uncle the first time, God brought this topic up again. This time, God spoke to me about forgiving not only my uncle's actions but also the effects those actions had on my life." Her life was smeared with the ripple effects of his selfish actions, and she needed to forgive him for those ripples to find healing and freedom.

It can be painful to forgive, but we must ask ourselves, *Do I want to forgive as I have been forgiven?* On one occasion many years ago, I was unable to attend a meeting of a woman's leadership council of which I was a member.

Many in the group took advantage of my absence to slander me. The woman I sent to the meeting in my stead later informed me of the verbal butchery that had taken place. I was stunned. It was as if someone had plunged a dagger into my gut.

After a few weeks, when the dust had settled in my emotional framework, I went to the council director and asked her about what my friend had reported. I made a point of sharing how it made me feel. She agreed that she was wrong to allow this attack to occur, taking responsibility and asking for my forgiveness. I forgave her, but I still felt the sting of the hurt.

After this conversation, I realized how emotionally arduous it was to forgive. Even though I genuinely meant what I said when I forgave her, I still felt shamed, sliced and diced emotionally. Forgiving the collective group took me some time as I had to process the sin against me. Finally, God did bring me to a sincere place of forgiving these women. Forgiveness, in effect, means that we hurt twice—once during the actual offense, and again whenever the hurt arises during the forgiveness process. Like Terri, I learned that to experience true freedom I must forgive not only the actions of those who hurt me but the effects of their actions.

It took me some time, my friend. But who am I, really? I am a forgiven sinner like them. I make mistakes. Jesus taught me to forgive others as I have been forgiven, but I am still growing in this! How about you? How are you doing with forgiving others? If we want to truly experience

His forgiveness and step into a redemptive lifestyle, we must forgive.

BEFORE WE GO ON

In this chapter we have looked at three sides of forgiveness:

1. Sin separates all humans from God. We all need forgiveness. And we are forgiven for all of our sin through Christ's death on the cross.

2. Even though we are forgiven, we continue to live life and we continue to sin. Christ calls us to approach Him with our sin on a daily basis, sincerely confessing our sin and receiving His cleansing forgiveness.

3. We can expect that others will sin against us. And as women who know forgiveness for our personal sin, we have the opportunity and need to forgive others who have sinned against us!

Out of these truths, pray over and journal about these three questions:

1. Do you know for sure and are you truly able to celebrate the forgiveness for all your sin that Jesus covered by His death on the cross? Are you assured that you have eternal life? (See 1 John 5:11-13.)

2. Are you living out a redemptive lifestyle, daily confessing your sin and receiving the cleansing forgiveness of Christ? (See 1 John 1:9.)

3. Is there someone who has wounded you or sinned against you whom you need to forgive? (See Luke 11:4.)

Take some time with the Lord and pray over each of these aspects of forgiveness, asking Him to show you what He wants to concentrate on with you. Begin journaling as Jesus uncovers where in these three aspects of forgiveness you might move forward.

Finally, like our courageous girlfriend in Luke 7, let us triumphantly be sent on our way as we live forward in His magnificent provision of forgiveness, hearing Jesus gently say to each of us, "Go in peace" (Luke 7:50).

———————————

Father, this foundational reality of receiving Your forgiveness and forgiving others who wound us is our joyful reality—yet it can be so painful. To know we are forgiven brings us to such a high point in our lives. We praise You that as we experience Your forgiveness on a daily basis, You send us into life with Your peace and steadfast love. We are humbled to realize that as we have been forgiven, so shall we compassionately offer forgiveness to those who sin against us. Help us, Lord, to live a redemptive lifestyle, quick to continue in Your forgiveness as well as to forgive others. Amen.

 ## DISCIPLEMAKER CHALLENGE

- Do you experience a deep assurance of Christ's forgiveness in your heart and life?

- How do you live out being forgiven and forgiving others in your life today?

- As you step in to discipling another woman, how do you think it might affect her growth if she has not embraced the all-encompassing forgiveness of her sin through Christ?

CHAPTER TWO

We Are Safe

In peace I will lie down and sleep. L ORD, you alone keep me safe.
⤷ PSALM 4:8

Through faith you are kept safe by God's power. ⤷ 1 PETER 1:5

They aren't afraid when bad news comes. They stand firm because they trust in the L ORD. ⤷ PSALM 112:7

THIS DAY WAS NOT like other June days in Colorado Springs. The sun was ablaze. We had been experiencing overwhelming heat in the midst of a long-term drought. Our one-month-old garden and landscape was greening up and flourishing thanks to our vast sprinkler systems, but on this day as I vacuumed our home and prepped to go spend some time with our two grandsons I noticed an orange twinge in the air outside. The smell of smoke and an incandescent haze seemed to come from the west of us.

I did not hear sirens.

I thought, *Something is burning somewhere.* As I drove to our son's home to pick up the boys, I caught sight of the problem. Just over the ridge of the foothills, massive flames were spewing up and out of the canyon.

No sirens yet.

When I picked up the boys from their neighbors, they went ballistic at the sight of the blaze shooting up. We huddled close in the driveway, and I prayed that God would take care of us, their parents, their neighbors, and their friends. "Jesus, keep us all safe." Still feeling somewhat stunned, we went back into their neighbors' home and sat with them, viewing the "live" report: "Not under control. Not sure how it started. Firefighters are having a difficult time getting to this fire."

Not sure?

Still no sirens?

Two days and nights passed. The fire, still not contained, began to spread to areas around the canyon. Several structures were lost. Fire commanders and their teams were working night and day to keep the surrounding communities safe. But an uncanny sense of doom filled the conversations and posture of those of us who lived there.

Three days after this fire started it went out of control. It blew up and out of the canyon and over the foothills toward our homes.

At last we heard sirens.

We evacuated. The scene was apocalyptic. The billowing clouds of smoke were stained a luminescent blood orange as they descended over our neighborhoods.

I am grateful that my husband was out of the country. Normally, I would count on Tom during moments like these. But instead, as the fire made its way toward our home, Christ's inner presence gave me an ability to move in quiet strength as I faced multiple decisions and interactions. I was bolstered with a strong sense of courage.

We were now members of a broad community given orders to evacuate. After several decisive discussions via cell phone with my husband, I packed a few precious items, closed up our home, and headed out of town with my son and his family.

As our three cars caravanned south on the interstate, I took one last look in the direction of the descending inferno. Though the impending destruction was falling upon homes of neighbors and friends, Christ calmed my spirit. I heard Him say almost audibly, *Don't look back. I will keep you safe.* I turned away from a scene that wanted to hold my gaze and create fear in my heart.

And then, much to my surprise, I began to sing some of my favorite songs that I learned as a child. I am not a musical person, nor do I normally express myself through song. But there I was, singing, of all things. A wave of calm came over me as my own voice serenaded me on my way: "Every day with Jesus is sweeter than the day before. Every day with Jesus I love Him more and more. Jesus saves and keeps me, and He's the one I'm living for. Every day with Jesus is sweeter than the day before."[8]

Why was I singing? Why was I relaxed? Why was there a deep rolling joy flowing throughout my body? Because in

Christ I was safe! I knew that no matter what happened, Jesus would take care of us.

A month before the fire I had memorized Psalm 121:

I will lift up my eyes to the mountains;
From where shall my help come?
My help comes from the LORD,
Who made heaven and earth.
He will not allow your foot to slip;
He who keeps you will not slumber.
Behold, He who keeps Israel
Will neither slumber nor sleep.

The LORD is your keeper;
The LORD is your shade on your right hand.
The sun will not smite you by day,
Nor the moon by night.
The LORD will protect you from all evil;
He will keep your soul.
The LORD will guard your going out and your
    coming in
From this time forth and forever.

PSALM 121, NASB

In the days following the fire, these strong gracious words would come to mind after we returned from evacuation, and I was reminded that God indeed was my keeper. He had kept me, my children, and our homes safe.

DESPERATE FOR SAFETY

Safety in Christ is a spiritual awareness of His presence in us and alongside us as we face every circumstance in life. The fact that we are not in control and have never been in control of our lives pushes us to abandon ourselves to the One who is sovereign and never taken by surprise by any of our life situations. And as we disciple another, having a bedrock assurance that we are safe will embolden us to share Christ and His Word with enormous confidence! Because we are in Christ and His Spirit dwells in us, we can rely on Him at any given moment. When we walk through upheaval, we learn to rest in Him, knowing that we are in the hands of the One who has the power to either change the circumstances or keep us as we walk into the midst of tragedy, loss, and fear.

Rahab knew what it was like to face the complete desolation of her city and move forward in faith and confidence. But because she recognized the great God of Israel and desired to trust only in Him, she was saved and brought into a new life even as her city was completely destroyed.

Rahab's story starts in the Old Testament of the Bible, and the stunning legacy of her faith gave her a place in the New Testament as well. Like our friend from the last chapter, she was a prostitute who came to faith. Eagerly, and trusting that the God of Israel would protect her, she entrusted herself to the mercy of the men of God. And as she suspected and hoped for, this God of the Israelites was faithful to His Word.

What draws me to Rahab is that no one around her had a saving faith. No one around her had entrusted themselves to the living and powerful God. But when Rahab learned of all that the God of Israel was doing, she was awestruck. Something within this prostitute's soul longed for a way out of her situation. Can you feel her desperation? Providentially the spies from Israel came to her neighborhood. Rahab risked it all and asked them to save her from the life she had and the impending destruction of her home city, Jericho. She transferred her trust to a God who could move her from her desperate, degrading existence to an uncharted land and life of promise.

So even before Christ came, we see that God offered a life of safety and belonging to anyone who trusted in Him. Rahab's choice to risk it all by faith moved her from a life of prostitution to a life of great faith and fruitfulness. That her step of faith would leave such a legacy probably did not even enter her mind the day God delivered her from the destruction of Jericho. And the Bible teaches us that Rahab's legacy blesses even us today.

GO DEEPER

Rahab's story in Scripture helps us immerse ourselves in this idea of safety in our God. Let's take a closer look at her story in the book of Joshua. Read the verses in your favorite translation, then answer the questions in your journal.

Read Joshua 2:1-24

As you go through the passage, consider this question: If you were in Rahab's situation, what choices might you have made?

Verse 1

1. Why did the two spies come to Jericho?

Verses 2-7

2. Why do you think the king came to Rahab with his search?

3. Why do you think Rahab lied? (Verses 9-11 might help here.) What would you have done?

Verses 8-14

4. What did Rahab say to the two spies that showed she had faith in their God?

5. What appeal did Rahab make to the two spies?

6. What do you think motivated Rahab to trust these two men?

7. What do you learn about Rahab's character as you examine the details of her request?

Verses 15-24

8. What is the deal she struck up with these spies?

9. How do you think Rahab felt as she tied the red cord in her window? What does this red cord represent?

Read Joshua 6:20-25

Verses 20-21

10. Describe what was going on in the city as Rahab and her family waited for the two spies to keep their promise. What do you think their hearts were

going through and that their conversation might have been during this period of waiting?

Verse 22

11. What did Joshua command the two spies to do?

Verses 23-25

12. Why is Joshua's and the two spies' faithfulness so remarkable?

13. Imagine you are part of Rahab's family as they escape. What emotions might you experience?

14. Do you think Rahab had a true faith in God? Why or why not?

15. What do you think the red cord came to represent for Rahab and her family?

16. What safety was offered to Rahab and her family? Compare with Deuteronomy 7:1-3. According to this mandate, what should have happened to Rahab and her family? What does the safety offered to Rahab and her family reveal about God's heart? (See 2 Peter 3:9.)

Read Hebrews 11:31

17. Why is Rahab remembered for her faith in Hebrews 11:31?

Read James 2:24-26

18. Why did James point to Rahab as an example of the proper outworking of faith and works?

Read Matthew 1:5-6, 16

19. Who was Rahab's son?

20. What do you know about Boaz? (See Ruth 2:1, 4, 8; 4:13, 21.)

21. Rahab was in the lineage of Jesus. We often think about Mary the virgin mother of Jesus when we consider His lineage, but here is a former

prostitute given a place of honor! What do you learn about God through this privilege given to her?

22. What was the ultimate legacy of Rahab?

23. How are we blessed today because of her faith?

SAFETY IN UNCERTAINTY

You are safe! When we hear Christ speak this foundational reality into our lives, something deep within us longs to step into that certainty. Assurance of our safety is ours if we have entrusted our lives to Christ.

Now, you may be thinking of the story of the fire I told at the beginning of the chapter. Sure, my home was safe, but didn't some people lose their homes? Yes, they did. In fact, 347 homes were destroyed in that fire. And some of those homes belonged to close friends of mine.

This is a hard truth: safety in Christ does not mean that circumstances and relationships always go the way we want.

You might be thinking, *How can we be "safe" if we can't control the outcome of uncertain life circumstances?* We need to recognize this: we are never in control, we were never in control, and we will never be in control.

We completely deny this when things are going well. We simply do not realize how out of control we actually are. And usually when complications arise we hope to "regain" some control. Interesting, isn't it? The fact is that we were never in control even when life was "normal." It is virtually impossible to regain something you never had in the first place.

This truth can lead us to desperation deep within our souls and affect every aspect of our lives if we do not confront the impact it has on us. We do not need to live one more day with this dominating anguish within us.

The common misbelief of being in control can lead us to wrong conclusions about our lives and especially about God. That is why this foundational reality that *we are safe* is so critical. When we clasp on to the reality that our safety is *in Christ*, the "blessed controller of all things" (1 Timothy 6:15, *Phillips*), regardless of our circumstances, we can find increased joy and authenticity in our walk!

The enemy of this world would have us bend in fear as we face the unexpected in our lives. Christ would have us hold His gentle strong hand as we face the unexpected.

My father died of brain cancer in 2000. My dad was a genius. He had been a NASA engineer. So why would God allow the very part of him that was so accomplished be taken from him during the end of his life? Although Dad could still talk, laugh, and live at home after the cancer treatment, he had to deal with a reduced intellect. Thinking seemed laborious, and even the simplest cognitive processes refused to flow smoothly.

I went to spend some time with him shortly before his death. One day, he and I were sitting in the kitchen, mulling over what he would have for lunch. I just had to ask him, "Dad, do you know what is happening to you?" His eyes filled with a distant unfamiliar blankness. But somehow he understood what I was asking him. He bowed his head in a moment of reflection, then looked up and responded, "You know, Dana, I don't know . . . but Jesus knows." It was as if he brought me into his failing world and shared with me his sense of safety in Christ. His loss of intellect did not remove his faith.

There will be many painful challenges in life that we will not understand, but, as my dad testified, "Jesus knows." Jesus wants those who follow Him to know they are safe:

> My sheep listen to my voice. I know them, and they
> follow me. I give them eternal life, and they will
> never die. No one will steal them out of my hand.
> My Father, who has given them to me, is greater
> than anyone. No one can steal them out of my
> Father's hand. I and the Father are one.
>
> JOHN 10:27-30

What a comfort to know that Jesus and the Father are one. What a comfort to know that to be safe in Jesus' hand is to be safe in the Father's hand. No one can remove us from this safe place!

Like Rahab, we have gained all that God graciously bestows on those whom He loves. The shame, woundedness, wrong choices, or serious failures we have experienced no longer define us or have dominion over us. By faith in Christ our life is made new (see 2 Corinthians 5:17). We have walked straight out of our "Jericho," and by the miraculous power of God we have a new life ahead.

So what is your Jericho? Have you ever thought about the fact that you have absolutely no control over the events of your life? Where are you in your understanding and employment of this wonderful foundational reality? Where would you like to be? What do you think keeps you from resting in Christ when the unexpected happens?

Jesus understands. He knows what it is like to face the most difficult of circumstances, even death. He understands what it is like to feel alone as we enter into traumatic moments, days, or years. Jesus does not say He will remove the difficulties, but He does promise to be with us and gives us His peace in the midst of them.

Lord, for all of us . . . help us to grow in our quickness to respond to the unexpected with trust in You. . . . Remind us that You hold our hand . . . that You gently lead us in your amazing love for us. And that we are safe. Amen.

BEFORE WE GO ON

So far in our study we have moved from the deep spiritual reality that we are forgiven to the wonderful blessed reality that because we are forgiven, we are safe! As we forgive others and receive God's forgiveness, resting in His ongoing provision of safety, we will grow in our God-dependence in a way that will release within us His joy and peace as we walk in our world. We will grow in awareness that we belong to Him. We will find ourselves unabashedly asserting that we are beloved daughters of the King, resilient members of His family.

DISCIPLEMAKER CHALLENGE

- How might ongoing anxiety and fears that control your heart impact your ability to disciple others?

- How might you grow stronger in your sense of safety as you move through your daily life?

CHAPTER THREE

We Have Access

The Spirit gives life; the flesh counts for nothing. The words I have spoken to you—they are full of the Spirit and life. ⤴ JOHN 6:63, NIV

All Scripture is inspired by God and profitable for teaching, for reproof, for correction, for training in righteousness; so that the man of God may be adequate, equipped for every good work. ⤴ 2 TIMOTHY 3:16-17, NASB

We have a high priest who can feel it when we are weak and hurting. We have a high priest who has been tempted in every way, just as we are. But he did not sin. So let us boldly approach God's throne of grace. Then we will receive mercy. We will find grace to help us when we need it. ⤴ HEBREWS 4:15-16

It is through Him that we both [whether far off or near] now have an introduction (access) by one [Holy] Spirit to the Father [so that we are able to approach Him]. ⤴ EPHESIANS 2:18, AMP

THIS IS NOT A TAXI. My husband and I traded a wordless look. The friendly Indonesian driver smiled enthusiastically as we approached the sorry dilapidated 1950s station wagon. My husband, Tom, and our seven-year-old son, Michael, took their places in the front seat by the driver. The heat and humidity in Jakarta, Indonesia, were overwhelming—and the taxi had neither air conditioning nor windows that rolled down. Since there were no car seats or seat belts, our two younger children secured their heads in my lap in the back seat. Our stacked baggage loomed from the rear of the battered station wagon, threatening to fall on top of us at every bump, turn, or stop. As we made our way on the six-hour drive, I stared at the winding half-paved mountain roads lined with small villages. I felt as if I were encountering a National Geographic documentary right before my eyes.

God had called us to a country where we didn't know the language, the customs, or the people. We found ourselves killing rats and spraying cockroaches incessantly. We seemed to eat from a bottomless bowl of rice. Each day offered fluctuating emotional experiences both circumstantially and relationally.

My heart was in turmoil. One day I turned to a friend and declared, "If I am able to live here long term, it will have nothing to do with me. I will be here if and only if Jesus keeps me here!"

We ended up living in Indonesia for almost eleven years. In the midst of cultural dissonance and what seemed like continual adjustment, I decided to reject the idea of isolating myself and "holding my breath" until we went back to America. After two years of learning language and culture, I wrote in my journal, "Lord, I don't want to survive here . . . I want to thrive here!"

I had been in Indonesia long enough to know that I could not do this alone. I needed to live continually out of the abundance available to me by accessing my heavenly Father through prayer, His Word, and His Spirit.

The woman who discipled me a few years before had taught me about these three means of access, and from her life and teaching I had learned that they were not just options but necessary for a vibrant life in Christ. But it was so easy to avoid them when I was "stressed"!

I made a decision.

No matter what, every morning I was going to sit on our bed, Bible in hand, and not move into my day until I had prayed and truly met with Jesus in His Word. This sweet time with Him would help me follow His Spirit's leading throughout my day. Implementing this decision was not easy. There were interruptions to this commitment now and then. But overall, since 1986, I have found that God has supernaturally supported me and helped me to put this choice into action.

Although this was an important choice for me, my heavenly Father helped me understand that it was just as, if not more, important to Him. We cannot even begin to comprehend God's love for us. He provides these means of access for our benefit, but at the heart of it, God desires fellowship with us!

When we meet with God in His Word, through prayer, or through following His Spirit, we cultivate a communion with Him that will sustain us deeply. As beloved daughters of the King, we are entitled to enjoy access to the Creator and Blessed Controller of the universe. But we must make the effort. It is time to flee our excuses as we take God up on His offer of access. This isn't discipline for discipline's sake. If we do not intentionally alter our daily agenda, we can bankrupt our desire to live out an authentic faith.

BE BOLD!

Once again, we can look at a woman in Scripture who helps us understand this idea of access to God. This woman, whose name we do not know, teaches us much about determination, willpower, and motivation to access Jesus in complete trust and abandonment. You may have heard this story many times, but have you considered the courage it must have taken for her to approach Jesus?

When I hear that this woman had a sickness that made her "bleed," I am immediately taken back to my younger years when I felt both physically and emotionally miserable for almost two weeks a month. This precious woman bled for twelve years (imagine having a twelve-year-long period!), and no one could help her. She must have felt very weak due to anemia, and whenever she stood up she may have dealt with dizziness. No doubt a putrid smell followed her wherever she went. If I were in her shoes, how I smelled might have inhibited my trudging forth as she did through the throng surrounding Jesus. And this woman, because of the Judaic laws, was ceremonially unclean, which meant she was not permitted to take part in the temple ceremonies and could make someone else unclean just by touching them. This made her an exile among her own people (see Leviticus 15:19).

She was an outcast, and she had spent all of her money looking for medical assistance. So imagine her relief when she heard about Jesus! Imagine the excitement and hope she must have felt, knowing that the Healer-Savior was near! Because she had heard of the things He had done, she trusted that she could access Him for help. Because of who He was, she was convinced she needed only to touch His clothes. And so she did.

That she was instantly healed is miraculously significant. But what astonishes me is that Jesus, even though He was in the midst of a pack of people pressing in on Him, was aware that this woman had approached Him. The omniscience (all-knowing nature) of Jesus and omnipotence (all-powerful nature) of Jesus cannot be hidden in this passage. And because she gained access, power had gone out from Him to her. He knew that she had risked it all. In pursuing access to the Savior, she proved her faith in Christ to be authentic.

Jesus stopped at this woman's bold approach. He made everyone wait. What this woman had done merited attention. Jesus honored her determined spirit of faith and action by calling her out of the crowd. Knowing that she could not hide from Him, she "fell at his feet . . . shaking with fear" (Mark 5:33). This action was a breakthrough moment for her. Others whom Jesus had healed had left Him without even saying thank you—and this woman fell at His feet. Jesus' final word to this woman was, "Dear woman, your faith has healed you. Go in peace. You are free from your suffering" (v. 34).

Take note! Not once did Jesus reprimand her for breaking Judaic ceremonial laws. Not once did He belittle her for assuming that she could approach Him. No—rather, He affirmed her boldness. He honored her desire to access Him.

📖 GO DEEPER

This woman's story helps us understand the profound beauty of our access to God. Read Mark 5:21-34 in your favorite translation, then answer the questions in your journal. Pay particular attention to the setting, the players, and the plotline before and after this woman was healed. Place yourself in her shoes. Would you have approached Jesus?

Verses 21-24

1. Consider first what we learn about Jairus and his daughter. Why do you think Jesus was going with Jairus to his house when we know He could have healed his daughter from anywhere?

2. Do you think it unusual that a synagogue ruler would request Jesus' help? Why?

3. Imagine you are the woman with the hemorrhage in this passage. Would this

crowd of people heading toward Jairus's home hinder you from approaching Jesus? Why or why not?

Verses 25-26

4. Describe the woman's need. What might she have been feeling?

Verse 27

5. What do you think she had heard about Jesus? How might she have heard about Him as an outcast?

Verses 28, 34

6. Why do you think she felt she needed to just touch His clothes? Why would she have tried to touch His clothes rather than approach Him directly?

7. What does Jesus explain was the reason He healed her?

Verse 29

8. Describe a time when you trusted God and saw Him intervene to take care of you. What did you learn about God because of this?

9. The story of the "bloody woman" is told also in Matthew 9. If we fast forward to Matthew 14:36 we find that, perhaps, this woman's story had spread: "They begged him to let those who were sick just touch the edge of his clothes. And all who touched his clothes were healed." Have you ever seen God's work in another's life and hoped for the same? Or have you observed God's work in your life touch others? What was the result?

Verse 30

10. What do we learn about gaining access to Jesus based on His reaction here?

Verse 31

11. What do we learn about gaining access to Jesus based on the disciples' reaction in this verse?

12. Have people ever tried to dismiss what happens when you access Jesus and see Him do amazing things? Have you ever tried to dismiss someone else's experience in accessing Jesus? Why do you think we as humans do this?

13. Do you ever feel like your reasons for approaching Jesus are too insignificant relative to the needs of others? If so, why? If not, what other things might hinder you from approaching Him?

Verse 32

14. Do you think Jesus did not know who had touched Him and been healed? If not, why do you think He asked this question? Why do you think He persisted in setting this woman apart?

Verse 33

15. How do you think this woman felt as Jesus called her out? What did she do that reflected her deep reverence and gratefulness to Jesus?

16. How did this experience of approaching Jesus by faith deepen her trust in Him?

Verse 34

17. How do you think the faith of Jairus was affected as he watched and waited while this woman approached Jesus?

18. As He did with the woman in Luke 7, Jesus sent her away gently. Compare the parting comments Jesus made to both of these women (Mark 5:34; Luke 7:50). How do you think those words impacted them long-term? Do you reflect on certain words from Scripture to quiet your heart and encourage you to keep walking out life by faith?

PURSUING ACCESS

This woman had access to Jesus in a way that we don't—she could reach out and physically touch Him. But God knows we need to "touch His garment" as she did—to feel His presence and power and hear Him speak gently to us. So what are our means of access today?

1. Prayer

Prayer is God's idea. In prayer, God bids us to connect with Him intimately and in a conversational way so that we might know Him more deeply. The Scriptures teach us to pray about everything and without ceasing (1 Thessalonians 5:17-18). And though praying regularly and consistently seems to make sense and is a desire we have, many of us do not take God up on this precious means of access. As pastor F. B. Meyer noted, "The greatest tragedy of life is not unanswered prayer, but unoffered prayer."[9] Like the bloody woman in Mark 5, we need to grasp that we are desperate and make every effort to approach Jesus regularly!

Jeremiah 33:3 and Philippians 4:6-7 are my favorite verses on prayer. In Jeremiah 33:3, God invites us to pray, promising that He will answer and show us great and mighty things. To me this means there are no limits on what I can bring to my Father and that His resources to answer me are limitless!

Philippians 4:6-7 speaks right to a common angst most of us experience—anxiety. As a woman, wife, mom, grandma, daughter, sister, and friend, I often find myself needing to take Philippians 4:6-7 to heart. Despite how weak we might feel at our most anxious moments, we are boldly exhorted in this verse to not be anxious about anything! Why? Because we are taught that, as we take all matters to God in prayer with thanksgiving, He will surround both our hearts and minds with His enduring peace. Leaving our needs and concerns at the feet of Jesus as we pray is God's antidote to anxiety.

Knowing that we have a God who invites us to approach Him and is limitless in His resources will keep our hearts and minds calm and trusting. Because of this, as we disciple women we must be faithful to pray for them and with them so they may learn how to trust God more deeply.

Are we approaching God in prayer through Christ regularly? Is prayer at the top of our priority list? Do we, like the bloody woman, expect that Jesus will engage with us?

2. God's Word

The Word, simply put, is God's written communication and revelation of Himself to us. God discloses Himself throughout His Word, from Genesis to Revelation. As we spend daily time in Scripture, He personally reveals Himself to us as the multifaceted God He is! The Word of God is the most tangible of our three means of access.

We must not take it lightly that God's Word is inspired. Second Timothy 3:16 clearly tells us that "all Scripture is inspired by God" (NLT). The original Greek word for *inspired* is *theopneustos*, which means "given by inspiration of God" or "breathed into by God."[10] When we engage with God's

Word, we are putting ourselves in an expectant posture to hear God speak.

Numbers 23:19 reminds us that "God isn't a mere human. He can't lie. He isn't a human being. He doesn't change his mind. He speaks, and then he acts. He makes a promise, and then he keeps it." So when we access God through His Word, we are not hearing from an "imaginary force" or someone who is just like us—we are hearing from the almighty God! We are listening to the One who cannot lie, who does not change His mind, and who keeps His promises. In a world where no one seems to keep their word, we can have confidence in our honest, steadfast, faithful God.

As we disciple women, we want to talk about God. The Bible allows God to speak for Himself. It is our responsibility to bring Him to the table.

Are you captivated by the fact that as you are in His Word you are engaging directly with the living God? Are you aware that when He speaks He will not lie? When your heavenly Father makes a promise He will keep it!

3. The Holy Spirit

The Holy Spirit, God Himself living in those who believe, brings prayer and the Word to life (1 Corinthians 3:16). The Spirit took up residence in us the moment we transferred our trust to Christ, personally sealing us and protecting what God promises to those who belong to Him (Ephesians 1:13). When we don't know what to pray, He prays for us (Romans

8:26). He brings understanding to Scripture as we read and meditate on it. His Spirit draws us, guides us, and changes us to be like Christ (John 14:17, 26). We must not only be aware of Him in us but also hear and obey His voice as He leads us. As Watchman Nee admonishes us from his book, *The Normal Christian Life*,

> Living in the Spirit means that I trust the Holy Spirit to do in me what I cannot do myself. This life is completely different from the life I would naturally live of myself. Each time I am faced with a new demand from the Lord, I look to him to do in me what he requires of me. It is not a case of trying but of trusting; not of struggling but of resting in him.[11]

The woman who was healed of her blood disease did not need to rely on the Holy Spirit because she was physically present with and experienced the living Christ. But we have His Spirit *in us*. As we disciple women, we need to listen to the Spirit's guidance as we meet with them and faithfully urge them to seek Him and obey His leading.

When I was in my twenties I was often depressed. I saw that people were going to let me down, even those who said they loved me, like my husband, family, and friends. I needed to know that God loved me, no matter what. As I was in **His Word** God spoke through Jeremiah 31:3, telling me that He loved me with a different love than all the people in my life—an everlasting love. I **prayed** and thanked Him for the amazing sense of His care for me that I felt at that moment. And whenever those around me let me down, **His Spirit** would remind me and woo me back to the great, amazing love that He has for me. When we activate these three means of access through our daily choices, they will naturally integrate and flow within us day by day, deepening our relationship with God.

BEFORE WE GO ON

Utilizing these three means of access cultivates the attachment every disciple longs for. When we truly access Christ through prayer and the Word, allowing His Spirit to fill us daily, we grow in our ability to take hold of His thoughts and His ways and increase in wisdom. The world cannot offer us anything like this sustaining connection with God. Living apart from Jesus because we do not access Him will be lonely, disappointing, and empty. For ourselves and those we disciple, this one foundational reality—*we have access*—is indispensable.

Think about your life and the privilege of access you have to God. The frequency with which we approach and access Jesus is directly proportionate to the sense of security we experience in our lives. If you felt a bit wobbly at the knees when we considered the foundational reality that *we are safe*, perhaps it is because you are not sure of what Jesus promises us. Perhaps God is imploring you to move toward Him as you never have before. Perhaps He is urging you to meet with Him daily in His Word and prayer, both consistently and continually.

What hindrances, excuses, or daily challenges tend to suffocate your desire to truly set apart time to sit with Jesus? What lies entrap you when you allow other activities to crowd out your opportunity to daily access Christ? Are these distractions really worth the cost of losing out on intimacy with Jesus?

Pray over these distractions. Ask God to show you how temporal they are. What decisions will you make so you can take God up on His provision of access? What choices will you insist upon as you step forward in your pursuit of accessing Christ? What things will you let go? What things will you delay? What things will you add?

———————

Lord Jesus, like the precious woman with a blood disorder, we humbly fall at Your feet, realizing that You offer Yourself to us, desiring to bring us close to You so that we might know You. Like this woman facing the crowd, we come up against distractions that tend to get in our way. We want to be women who expectantly meet with You and hear from You. We want to be women who listen to and obey Your Spirit. We want to be women who insist on spending time with You. Help us to reorganize our lives so that we can access You daily. Guard us from the evil one who is of this world, who wants to suffocate us with daily expectations and requirements that in comparison to You are worthless. Amen.

📜 DISCIPLEMAKER CHALLENGE

- Why do you think that as a discipler it is vitally important that you daily spend time with Jesus in the Word and prayer?

- What limitations would the one whom you disciple experience if she is not daily accessing Christ?

- Discipling is about helping someone attach deeply to Christ. How might studying the three means of access together with someone you are discipling cultivate her attachment to Him?

CHAPTER FOUR

We Are Becoming

You are our Father, we are the clay, and You our potter; and all of us are the work of Your hand. ❧ ISAIAH 64:8, NASB

God planned that those he had chosen would become like his Son. ❧ ROMANS 8:29

IT WAS A FEW DAYS after September 11, 2001.

I had been in Vancouver when terrorists attacked the World Trade Center. It had been impossible to get back into the United States for days—every airport was closed. But now, finally, I was in line to go through immigration from Canada to the US.

Everyone was on high alert. As I milled along in line to get my passport checked, I began making a mental to-do list of everything I had to get done once I got back to Colorado.

But once I stood before the immigration agent I started to get alarmed. He couldn't stop staring at my passport. Then it dawned on me. I had lived in Indonesia for more than ten years. Indonesia is a predominantly Muslim country. Not only that, but on this particular trip I'd had pepper spray confiscated at customs when I had entered the country.

The immigration agent scrutinized my face. "So, Mrs. Yeakley, tell me about this passport renewal in Jakarta, Indonesia," he said, his tone suspicious and intimidating. Did he see me as a threat?

In an instant I was severely flustered. "Uh, uh . . . I don't remember. My husband must have taken the train to Jakarta and renewed all of our paperwork." My lack of memory wasn't helping my case.

"Your husband." He squinted. "Oh, so there were two of you there?"

Anxious, I immediately looked to Jesus. I was still talking to the immigration agent, but I was also talking to Jesus.

Jesus, does he think Tom and I could possibly be terrorists?

"Well, yes." I had visions of them taking me to a back room to torture the truth out of me. "And our three kids . . . as missionaries."

He seemed to stiffen. The people in line behind me leaned in to listen.

"Yes." I smiled nervously. "For ten and a half years, sir."

Lord, do You see what is happening here?

"Wait here." He shifted away behind the curtain in order to speak with another person.

The next few moments seemed endless. I turned to the people behind me, gave another uneasy smile, and said, "Yikes!" I imagined being thrown into a Canadian prison and being stuck on trial for years.

But God was supervising my situation.

As each ridiculous possibility pressed in on me, I invited Jesus to intervene and help me to respond as He wanted me to.

Even in the midst of my anxiety, I sensed that Christ was helping me and at the same time growing my ability to face fear on my feet.

I felt it.

God was doing just as He had promised me in Proverbs 31:25: "Strength and dignity are her clothing, and she laughs at the time to come" (ESV). He had led me to that verse twenty-five years before, promising me right then and there, *You are a woman who laughs and has fun, but you are not a woman who can laugh at the future. I will strengthen you and increase your personal sense of dignity in such a way that you will truly be able to laugh at the time to come!*

In the next moment, the agent returned and stoically let me through the line.

Those fifteen minutes in my life may not seem like a big deal now. But I was feeling exceptionally vulnerable! In moments of helplessness and alarm, God poignantly steps in and shows me He is at work within my spirit. It is not comfortable in the moment, but this work brings maturity and peace in the long-term.

This wonder of "becoming," of growing and changing into all He desires for us as His beloved daughters, happens when we least expect it. God allows us to be put in weighty situations where He delivers us either from the circumstances or within them.

Vital to our "becoming" is the assurance that God, as our

loving Father, is always present and always in control. We can accept, fight, or flee His extraordinary plan for us to become like Christ. But the resonating truth is that in every situation He does have a plan for us—and it is good! Elisabeth Elliot wisely reminds us, "It is God to whom and with whom we travel, and while He is the end of our journey, He is also at every stopping place."

THREE PICTURES OF BECOMING

Did you know there are seven Marys mentioned in the New Testament? One of my favorite Marys is the sister of Lazarus and Martha. She offers us much to reflect on regarding this idea of "becoming." The reason I like this Mary so much is because she truly understood who Jesus was—even before others seemed to "get" Him. And the more time I have spent with Mary in the Scripture, the more I have come to realize how imperfect of a girlfriend she is! Nevertheless, God used Mary's life.

God never intended us to do everything that Mary did or become just like her. But the things He highlights through her choices and responses are beneficial for us to reflect on. As Mary models a woman who in innocence and faith became the woman God created her to be, so we too are invited to become all that God designed us to be!

In Scripture, we see Mary in three phases of her "becoming." The first phase is in Luke 10, when she sat at Jesus' feet, listening to and learning of Him. Her posture of desiring to listen and learn is contrasted against Martha's distraction. As women, we know the burden Martha felt. She bore the bulk of the workload, caring for their guests. But even though Martha's hard work is admirable, Jesus deliberately affirmed Mary's choice to sit at His feet.

In John 11, the second phase we see of Mary's "becoming," she was devastated and broken, falling at Jesus' feet when her brother, Lazarus, died. She had to face the fact that Jesus did not come through for her. By delaying His arrival, He let her brother die! Her emotions and faith were strained. Her reactions might lead us to conclude that this was not her best moment. But later, when her brother was miraculously raised from the dead and many people came to faith, Mary learned that the wisdom and timing of God is far beyond her ability to comprehend.

Finally, in John 12, we see Mary once again at Jesus' feet, exemplifying sincerity of worship and thankfulness. What Mary offered to Jesus in worship, He welcomed. While those around them denigrated Mary's actions as she worshiped Him, Jesus was the first to defend and affirm her demonstration of love. Mary had become a woman who was strong and resilient in her faith.

GO DEEPER

Read through each of the following scenes of Mary's "becoming" in your favorite translation, then answer the questions in your journal. Let Mary's words and actions speak for her as she becomes all God wants her to be!

Scene 1: Luke 10:38-42

Verse 38

1. Describe the scene as we enter into watching Mary relate to Jesus. What is Martha's role in this situation?

Verse 39

2. It was strange and even controversial for Mary to choose and be allowed to sit at Jesus' feet. She took "the place of a disciple by sitting at the feet of the teacher. It was unusual for a woman in first-century Judaism to be accepted by a teacher as a disciple."[12] And Mary stayed at His feet even when Martha threw a tantrum in front of the King of the universe! Christ affirmed and enjoyed Mary's choice. He endorsed Mary's awareness of who He truly was and her desire to grow spiritually. If you were literally sitting at Jesus' feet next to Mary, what would you ask Him?

Verses 40-41

3. Describe Martha's demeanor. What was she missing about the situation? How did Jesus help her understand what she was missing?

4. What advice would you give Martha so that she might find the freedom to sit at Jesus' feet despite the pressures of her valid hostess duties?

Verse 42

5. Jesus made a pointed conclusion here. Why do you think He did so?

6. In your own words, express what Jesus was saying to Mary and Martha in this verse.

7. In chapter 3 we talked about accessing Christ and insisting upon doing so in

our daily lives. If Jesus were to speak to you now about the importance of this choice, what might He say to you?

Scene 2: John 11:1-6, 17-45

Verses 1-2

8. Set the stage. Who were the players in this scene? Where were they? What was the situation?

Verse 3

9. How did the sisters describe Lazarus to Jesus in the message they sent Him? Describe the expectations they may have had as they sent for Him.

Verse 4

10. What was Jesus' response to their invitation?

Verse 5

11. Why is it important for us to know that Jesus loved the three siblings?

Verse 6

12. Why do you think Jesus delayed His coming to the sisters? (See v. 4 again.)

13. What do you think Jesus was indicating about His purpose regarding "becoming" for those He loves?

Verses 17-19

14. Describe the scene when Jesus arrived at Bethany. What do you think the sisters were feeling after losing their brother, Lazarus? Consider his cultural role as the man of their house and source of provision and protection.

Verses 20-27

15. What do we learn about Martha's personality in verse 20? Is Martha's

conversation with Jesus "heart to heart" or "head to head"? How does this help you to appreciate her relationship to Jesus?

Verses 28-33

16. Would you describe Mary's response in this scene as emotional or intellectual? Why? Was Mary a disciple? Explain your answer.

17. Please reread verses 20-33. These two sisters are very different! Note that both sisters said the same thing to Jesus when they met Him on His way. He responded differently to both, despite His equal love for them both (see v. 5). Compare His responses. What do we learn from Jesus' interaction with these two very different women as we think about our friends, family, and those we disciple? As we consider the idea of "becoming" in this chapter, what would you say was Jesus' intent in allowing Mary and Martha to go through this terrifying time? What was He building in their hearts?

Verses 34-37

18. Describe this scene. Though Mary and Martha were present, the emphasis shifts to the crowd. Why did Jesus cry?

19. What critique did some of the Jews offer?

Verse 38

20. Once again Jesus was "sad." Why do you think He felt sad after hearing the criticism of verse 37?

Verses 39-40

21. Jesus continued in conversation with Martha. What do you learn about both of them in this short exchange?

Verses 41-44

22. Read these verses out loud, with expression. What do you think the crowd, the sisters, and even Lazarus felt like?

23. What do you think Martha thought, especially after talking to Jesus about the resurrection in verses 23-26?

24. What do you think Jesus purposed that people would gain from this encounter?

25. Jesus directed them, "Take off the clothes he was buried in and let him go." Like Lazarus, we can be "buried"—under obstacles, misbeliefs, relational drain, and daily responsibilities that subtly burden us. As you hear these words that set Lazarus free, what comes to your mind about what might "bury" you? Perhaps Jesus wants to raise you up and set you free!

Verse 45

26. Many Jews put their faith in Jesus because of this miracle. What might Mary have felt as she experienced "becoming" right in front of them? What do you think Mary told them or shouted aloud as she experienced her brother coming back to life?

Scene 3: John 12:1-8

Verses 1-2

27. Describe the scene. What was the purpose of this dinner?

28. How do you think Martha felt when she received Jesus into her home this time? What might have been different from her experience and perspective in the first scene we looked at?

Verse 3

29. What did Mary do to honor/worship Jesus? What might Martha have been thinking?

30. How do you worship Jesus in your life?

Verses 4-6

31. How did Judas respond to Mary's loving worship of Jesus? How might others

respond to us when we want to freely worship or serve Christ as His Spirit leads?

32. What is crucial when we worship? How would you define worship (see also Romans 12:1)?

Verses 7-8

33. How did Jesus show support for Mary as Judas hypocritically opposed her actions?

34. How do you think Mary felt when Jesus defended her actions?

Reviewing the Scenes

35. What lesson do you learn from Mary as she chose to dismiss distraction and **sit at the feet of Jesus**?

36. What lesson do you learn from Mary as she in her disappointment **fell at Jesus' feet**?

37. What lesson do you learn from Mary as she in her gratefulness **anointed Jesus' feet**?

THE JOURNEY TO BECOMING

If Mary were sharing her experiences with us today, I think she would underscore three things for us to ruminate on when we talk about "becoming":

1. It is vital that we know and believe that Jesus loves us *always*! His love underscored His delay in coming to heal Lazarus. His stunning love outstretches our ability to comprehend it. Our response to His everlasting love must be trust.

2. Our journey to "becoming" will take twists and turns that we neither expect nor desire. Eventually, all of us come to a "trust" crossroads. We are allowed to take part in Mary's trust crossroad when her brother died. She, though thoroughly disappointed, ran out to meet Jesus and fell at His feet. Jesus felt her disappointment. He wept with empathy. Jesus longed that Mary, Martha, all their friends, and dissenting Jews would understand the greater purposes as to why He came. He ached that they would be able to simply trust His goodness for them.

3. As we accept His ways in our lives, all things, even those things in our past that wounded us or shamed us, are redeemed. He is working His long-term plan within us. "Becoming" lifts us up and out of our past. The process of becoming points us to Jesus, the blessed Controller of all things. God leads us through growth, developing in us Godlike responses to our disappointments, challenges, and times of disaster. His plan is that we become resilient women with a Christ-centered spirit.

Where we are in relation to this foundational reality that *we are becoming* is in a large way revealed by whether we "respond" to or "react" to life as it happens. We have a choice as to how we handle our life situations. Like Mary's dilemma of losing Lazarus, or my little parenthetic moment in the immigration line in Canada, whether we choose to respond or to simply react exposes our fears, our hopes, our needs, and our values.

When God allows disquieting incidents in our lives, often we simply react. Sometimes we grin and bear our way through crushing situations. Other times we panic. Allowing our reactions to overpower us reveals a lack of resilience and a weakness in faith. Have you ever reacted and flown off the handle at your spouse, the checkout girl, or another driver who pulls in front of you? Do you see your reactions? Do you like them?

We need to examine our lives for habitual reactions to situations and identify our coping strategies. Our reactions and the strategies spring from core lies we believe about ourselves or our lives. When we finally understand these lies, we have a choice to make. Will we continue to react, or will we repent and seek to respond in a godly way, taking action based on the truth?

Our firstborn, Michael, took the brunt of my immature reactions when I was in my mid-twenties. One incident in particular I have never forgotten.

I was overtired and expecting guests that evening. After straightening up our living room and preparing food in advance of their arrival, I sat down to catch my breath. Michael had just learned to crawl and loved the ground-level opportunities his new skill afforded him. And he could crawl fast! I watched him enthusiastically crawling about the room from where I sat—and then, with no warning, he bolted straight for the plant on the lower shelf of our small homemade bookcase. With delight he knocked the plant from the shelf, marveling at the power of his swing. The resulting explosion of dirt went everywhere—all around him and on him.

My reaction? Anger. With a raised voice and not a few sharp words, I let him know that I was displeased. His trembling pout turned into a loud cry of remorse. Immediately I felt distraught over my lack of control. Michael sobbed. He was acting like the ten-month-old that he was. I was not acting like the adult that I was!

I was deeply grieved. As Michael snuggled into my arms, seeking reassurance that all was well, I felt rather helpless. I had not and seemingly could not respond wisely and lovingly! My reactive outbursts were neither godly nor the way I wanted to be.

As I began to analyze my reaction in a very raw and prayerful way, God began to reveal the lies behind it. The first lie was that "my stuff is really important and must be protected at any cost." The second lie was that "in order to provide an enjoyable evening for our guests, I must have my home perfectly prepared." I valued "stuff" and "neatness" more than effectively parenting and truly loving Michael.

That day, my reaction and my one small step toward asking God for help set in motion transformational changes, and I have been "becoming" ever since!

Recently, we bought a new coffee table for our living room. It is the first time we have ever done so—because for years we had used an old trunk that we had shipped back from Indonesia! When we placed this new, fairly expensive piece in our living room, I actually had to interrogate myself: "Am I going to worry about keeping this piece of furniture looking new?" I had to tell myself the truth about this piece of furniture—that it really did not matter!

Within a week, my grandson was doing his homework on our new coffee table. He was figuring out the population of his birthplace during the year he was born. As I watched him press hard and write the number on his paper, I thought, *I wonder if bearing down like that as he writes will leave an impression in the wood?* Sure enough, as he lifted his pencil and paper, the numerals 10,600 were forever etched in my brand-new table.

When he saw it, he lightly said, "*Oops*—sorry, Grandma!" And my response, praise God, allowed me to see how God has been at work in my "becoming" since his dad was a baby. With sincere joy I told him, "Well, this is very special for me! I now have a memory of you instilled in this wood that will never go away!"

I really did mean what I said. (Although we did not use the table for homework after that!) Whenever I dust this coffee table, I am reminded of so many happy memories of helping Byron with his homework. God used this little episode to prove His work in me.

God desires for us to *respond* during intimidating life situations with alertness, peace, and resilience centered in Him. When we want to grow in our ability to respond like Christ, we must review the truth that not only did we receive eternal life when we initially trusted Christ but we have also received the promise of abundant life. We are becoming! And Christ invites us to make every effort to work out our becoming (see Philippians 2:12-13). Our effort in this means agreeing we have weaknesses that need His attention. Being aware of our ongoing growth as we disciple women keeps us humble and bolsters us to accept them as they encounter growth and change.

What habitual reactions cause you distress at this time in your life? Write a note to yourself about where you are in this process of "becoming." Pray over this note and surrender yourself to Jesus. Expect Him to come to your aid the next time you find yourself floundering in reaction instead of responding like Christ. And above all else, remember that you are loved by your Creator. His desire to work in you is for your benefit and His glory. Whether you seek His help or not, He loves you with unconditional, everlasting love!

Heavenly Father, knowing we are loved by You helps us to rest in Your protective shelter. Because we are loved, we want to respond to You in trust. Help us, Father, as we daily confront the abrasive stuff of life that pushes us toward reacting instead of responding like Christ. Open our spiritual eyes so we may see the strategies and lies our reactions are based on. Lord, in this area of learning

to respond, we want to joyfully and intelligently release
ourselves to you. Amen.

BEFORE WE GO ON

Now that we are at the end of our study of the four foundational realities that are basic to a genuine faith in Christ, what have you learned about yourself and your relationship with Him? My desire is that you would feel encouraged and empowered in your faith and that you would step into discipling other women as these truths sink deeply into your heart. And these four chapters can be studied together with someone you disciple!

In chapter 1 we celebrated that we are forgiven. We have been redeemed! With that said, we are aware that we continue to sin and are invited to daily repent and receive cleansing and forgiveness. Like the woman of Luke 7, we have heard Jesus say, "Your sins are forgiven. . . . Go in peace." As disciplers we must help others understand that they are forgiven and can live out a redemptive lifestyle.

Chapter 2 challenged us to review our lack of control over anything and everything in life. Like Rahab, we are assured that we are safe no matter what happens around us, despite our lack of control. Because we personally know the "blessed Controller of all things," we are protected as we face danger. To be safe does not mean we won't face difficulties or loss. "Safety" ultimately is an eternal status we hold as believers in Christ. And because "greater is He who is in you than he who is in the world" (1 John 4:4, NASB), we are guaranteed an unworldly sense of peace at all times. The women we will help also need to embrace this ongoing awareness that, no matter what, they are safe.

Chapter 3 reminded us that our finite human selves have access to the immortal, infinite, eternal God. Because God has offered us this access through prayer, His Word, and His active Spirit, we must consistently, boldly approach Him like our courageous friend who was instantly healed of her blood issues. We must incorporate these three venues of access into our daily lives, experiencing them as the lifelines to Christ that they actually are. The women we help must fully attach to Jesus and become independently dependent upon Him. We do a disservice to anyone we help if we do not impart the privilege of access that we as His beloved daughters have.

In chapter 4 we were awakened to God's wonderful work as we engage in the process of "becoming" all that He desires for us. Our greatest prospect as we grow toward perfection is to become like Christ. Mary's life of devotion to Jesus cast a model of becoming for us. As we remember that *we are becoming*, we must not forget that we, like those we disciple, are on a path to maturity. Writer and speaker Jill Briscoe has said that "we are to be models of growth, not models of perfection"[13] as we disciple others. For the women we come alongside, this aspect of discipleship allows us to sympathetically engage in their journey with them—because we are going through the same thing! What an honor to sit with another woman and encourage, challenge, and gently lead her as Christ transforms her into becoming all He has planned for her. As we personally submit to the wise, loving hand of our heavenly Father and grow, we will develop empathy toward those we come alongside and the wisdom to recognize the hand of God at work in their lives.

What amazing truth to take into our hearts: we are forgiven, we are safe, we have access, and we are becoming! With these foundational realties secured in our hearts and minds, let's move on to consider what it looks like to make disciples.

DISCIPLEMAKER CHALLENGE

- Are you personally aware of and gratefully entrenched in your process of becoming all that God wants for you?

- Are you growing in your ability to respond in a godly way to life's interruptions, difficult circumstances, or relationships?

- If the woman you disciple does not realize she has the capacity to respond in a godly way rather than to simply react, how might this affect her growth?

PART TWO

Make a Disciple

WHEN I FIRST ENGAGED in discipling women one-on-one, I always had to work through my own sense of inadequacy. I still feel a variety of misgivings to this day.

- Am I giving her what God says she needs? Or what she wants? Or what I want?
- Am I loving her and relating to her in the way God wants me to? And in a way that is helpful in each of our capacities and seasons of life?
- Am I aware of her struggles, concerns, fears, and hopes?
- Did I bring enough structure, enough relationship, enough prayer, enough of the Word when I met with her today? Did I talk too much?
- She didn't seem excited. What about her lack of interest?

- What about keeping track of what we have talked about and what she asked me to pray for?
- Am I praying enough for her?

Up until this point in our study of the gentle art of discipling women, we've been reminding ourselves of who we are in Jesus Christ for a very important reason: because only when we are secure in our relationship with Him can we truly find our footing as a discipler of women. We must answer this question: "Am I stepping into a God-ordained, God-empowered supernatural activity?" If we are—and indeed we are!—then we can rest in the One who will carry us as we disciple another woman. When we lose sight of this core truth about discipling, we will quickly turn and focus on our many inadequacies—and they will explode in our hearts and minds like shrapnel from a land mine.

We need to remember four distinct truths if we want to disciple women:

1. Making disciples is not a human idea. It is God's idea. When Jesus gathered His eleven disciples together after His resurrection and prior to His ascension, He appointed them to "go and make disciples" (Matthew 28:19). What amazing parting words! Along with those followers we have been especially invited into what God is already doing in the lives of women as we seek to disciple them.

2. At the core of discipling is a supernatural attachment.
   God involves Himself within the heart and life of the
   one we disciple. Remember our Webster definition of
   discipleship in the introduction of this book? Though
   helpful, it misses this crucial aspect of the discipling
   relationship. The Greek word Jesus used when He said,
   "Go and make disciples" is *matheteuo. Matheteuo* must
   be distinguished from the verb *matheo*, which was a
   common Greek word of the day. The word *matheo*,
   which is not found in the New Testament, means to
   solely learn without any attachment to the teacher
   who teaches. *Matheteuo*, by contrast, means not only
   to learn but to *become attached* to one's teacher and
   become his follower in doctrine and conduct of life.[14]
   For me, this word *matheteuo* completely separates discipling from any other mode of schooling or training.
   In college our professors practiced *matheo* with us.
   They were teachers who taught us, but they did not
   want (nor did we want) any "attachment" to them. As
   disciplers, however, we have the goal of attachment as
   we gently engage with those we help.

   So are we saying we want those we disciple to
   attach to *us*? Absolutely not! As we build a relationship and invest in someone it is not uncommon that
   some *might* subtly attach to us, and we need to be wary
   of letting that happen. Amy Carmichael, missionary
   to India for fifty-five years, knew this tendency: "If I
   slip into the place that can be filled by Christ alone,

making myself the first necessity to a soul instead of leading it to fasten upon Him, then I know nothing of Calvary love."[15] We desire the one we disciple to attach to the One we are both following: Jesus! Our role as discipler is to breed healthy attachment to Jesus.

3. As disciplers we are colaborers with God. We must correctly view ourselves this way when we disciple someone. Discipling another is never about us. In 1 Corinthians 3:3-9 Paul admonished those of the Corinthian church who distinguished themselves as followers of Paul or Apollos—because, though Paul and Apollos labored among the people of that church, it was God who made them grow.

This mentality should affect everything about my engagement as a discipler. For example, I must ally myself with God through prayer as I discern what I should be sharing with someone. I should not share only that which has changed my life (though there is a place for that). Even as I continue to meet with someone over a period of time, I must remain in alliance with God over their needs and growth, for it is God who makes them grow! This reality of discipling another frees me up in so many ways.

4. Making the choice to disciple women is a matter of obedience. Christ's words to His followers in Matthew 28:18-20 are not a suggestion. He is about to leave

them—and His words are brimming with insight into His vision for reaching the nations. He promises His authority and presence to those who carry out this command. As His daughter I want to obey Him. The beauty of this is that Jesus has not asked us to obey Him and do something without His complete assistance. As we obey Him we grow in the realization that His invitation is not to an impossible task but to a way of life!

WHAT DOES MAKING DISCIPLES LOOK LIKE?

A lot of times we use interchangeable terms for discipling like *mentoring, life coaching,* going to a *spiritual director,* or *counseling.* But discipling differs from these other relationships in some key ways. The main difference is wrapped up in the purpose and objective for the relationship.

Mentoring can mean a lot of things: all the way from helping someone to learn to cook, organize their home, raise kids, or play golf!

Life coaching typically involves focused help in career or personal challenges.

Going to a **spiritual director** involves self-focused interaction as one encounters the divine. A spiritual director usually charges an hourly fee.

Counseling targets certain aspects of one's personal, social, or psychological needs. A counselor also usually charges an hourly fee.

But as we disciple, our primary purpose is to come alongside the one we are discipling and intentionally build into her life as we share life, prayer, and His Word. Disciplemaking also includes the hope that the one we disciple also will eventually disciple someone else. Paul gave us this intentional vision in 2 Timothy 2:2: "You have heard me teach in front of many witnesses. Pass on to people you can trust the things you've heard me say. Then they will be able to teach others also."

Discipling is not a job we are hired to do or make money from. The choice to disciple others flows from our relationship with Jesus. This is where the true riches of the relationship come from. Matthew 10:8 offers us the posture we are to maintain as we disciple someone: "You have received freely, so give freely."

We have the opportunity to be generous from our heart as we disciple those God brings to us.

AM I QUALIFIED TO DISCIPLE?

A lot of us think of the following passage from the book of Titus when it comes to the idea of discipling women:

> Teach the older women to live in a way that honors God. They must not slander others or be heavy drinkers. Instead, they should teach others what is good. These older women must train the younger women to love their husbands and their children,

to live wisely and be pure, to work in their homes, to do good, and to be submissive to their husbands. Then they will not bring shame on the word of God.

TITUS 2:3-5, NLT

But what does it really mean to be an older woman? During the time of Jesus, the average life span of a woman was thirty-four years. So, then, who might be considered "older women" today? Every woman, no matter what her age, who is just barely a step ahead of another woman in her walk with Christ is an "older woman" and has the raw material to help another grow. Chances are that describes you! Know that God as already given you everything you need as you step into this art of discipling another woman.

GETTING PRACTICAL

Every artist needs to achieve excellence in the use of tools and skills required for their art—and since disciplemaking is an art, we need the proper tools and to develop the skills of our craft! In this second half of the book, we're going to dig into some practical questions about the discipling relationship, concentrating on the needed skills and practices of discipling:

- How do we create a life-giving atmosphere?
- Whom do we help?
- What do we share?
- How does discipling one-on-one actually work?

As we answer these questions, let us not forget that making disciples is always God's idea! We are being responsive to His command and will be completely supported and empowered by Him.

I pray that as we disciple, we would see the hand of God on the relationships He gives us. May He be glorified in our hearts and the hearts of those we disciple, and may those we help discover the joyous call to also go and disciple others!

CHAPTER FIVE

How Do We Create a Life-Giving Atmosphere?

We were gentle among you, like a nursing mother taking care of her own children. So, being affectionately desirous of you, we were ready to share with you not only the gospel of God but also our own selves, because you had become very dear to us. ❧ 1 THESSALONIANS 2:7-8, ESV

MY LONGTIME FRIEND, Cindy, lives in Chicago. I've always loved going to her house because it fills me with a sense of coming home. She has created an environment of relational warmth, comfort, and love. I feel safe there. And I am certain that many others have enjoyed her ability to create an atmosphere that draws people in and invites them to connect from the heart.

Healthy discipling relationships require a similar atmosphere. Like Cindy, whose home draws people to feel accepted and loved, we want to ensure a relational setting that will help those we disciple feel safe and cared for. None of us are just alike in how we disciple or in the atmosphere we offer and relate in. This is because all of us operate from the person God created us to be. We all have talents, skills, personality traits, relational strengths, and a desire to love. So let's think through and own the atmosphere that will flow from who each of us is and how God has wired us individually as we disciple others! Owning the atmosphere we offer will facilitate enjoyment, satisfaction, and growth for us and those we help.

PERSPECTIVE CHECK

Before we answer the question of how we create the right atmosphere, we must consider two key perspectives that inform the environment. These perspectives, which we see Jesus modeling in Matthew 9, can be boiled down to two questions: Do we see people, and are we willing to get involved with them?

Do We See People?

We will undergo a vision shift as we take on Jesus' heart for discipling. As our perspective matures, we begin to "see" people as He does. In the book of Matthew, we are given a glimpse of Jesus' heart as He sees the massive throng surrounding Him:

> *Seeing* the people, He felt compassion for them, because they were distressed and dispirited like sheep without a shepherd. Then He said to His disciples, "The harvest is plentiful, but the workers are few. Therefore beseech the Lord of the harvest to send out workers into His harvest."
>
> MATTHEW 9:36-38, NASB, EMPHASIS ADDED

Imagine yourself standing among the disciples at this moment. Do you see what a compassionate Savior Jesus is? He *sees* and compassionately responds to the many needy people around Him. Jesus teaches us a significant lesson at this crucial moment. He speaks to the distress of the people and identifies their greatest need: to know Christ and the salvation that only He offers. That is why Jesus came. Spiritual liberation provided only "in Christ" is at the crux of "the harvest," which, He notes, is plentiful.

Jesus directly connects the distressed and dispirited sheep before us to the great harvest of souls for which He came. What good is it to meet any other need if the greatest need is not met? As we begin to see people as Jesus sees people, we can then take part in the great adventure of laboring with Him. "Seeing" people as Jesus sees them is our ground zero as we step into discipling.

Recently my daughter, Amy, sent me these words after her morning walk around her neighborhood:

Look at me
See me
Listen to me
Hear me
Eyes peeking through patterned and tattered head scarf
Lips tight with wrinkles defining the years
Hands folded while briskly walking
Mismatched skirt loosely wrapped around a thin waist
Feet moving in worn out sandals seeking an unknown destination
Look at me
See me
Listen to me
Hear me
Dark twinkling eyes
Braided hair complete with colored clips bouncing while trying to stand still
A smile from ear to ear
Backpack held with firm and confident hands
Joyful, spirited, and eager for all the school day holds
Look at me
See me
Listen to me
Hear me
Clinging in fear of the buzzing bee
Jacket askew
Begging for anyone to protect from the ferocious stinger
Sweaty palms
Anxiety and distress

Look at me
See me
Listen to me
Hear me
Head down
Hands stuffed in pockets
Alone
When greeted posture changed and a light is turned on
Look at me
See me
Listen to me
Hear me[16]

I love how Amy articulated the need each person had to be seen and heard as she crossed paths with them. How about you? Do you "see" people? Before we can create an atmosphere that will serve those we disciple, we need to see people as Jesus sees them in the midst of a broken and harrowing world.

Will We Get Involved with People?

We might be busy with a variety of activities, but if we want to share in the heart of Jesus, we must relate to and invest in people like Jesus did.

This shift began to occur in my heart in 1975. I was involved in discipleship studies at Purdue University, and one night I attended a prayer focus with a small group of women. Our prayer guide had us pray over Matthew 9:36-38. I do not recall praying anything out loud. What I do recall is that as the prayers of others echoed around me, God began speaking to me in a quiet but commanding voice, asking me if I was willing to be one of those workers Jesus was talking about in Matthew 9.

My inner spirit trembled at the Holy Spirit's question. I was reluctant to surrender because I was aware of many stories that described how God was sending out workers around the world. I was not sure of what this would mean for my family. Honestly, I was concerned that I would have to leave home and serve overseas. But that night I quietly relinquished my future to His voice and over the next few years committed to learning about what it means to labor in His harvest. Although a major shift started in my heart during that prayer time, there was no instant change. God showed me and Tom the imperative need for our own personal growth and training before we could step out as laborers. And after it was all said and done, God did ask our family to go overseas, as I shared earlier. Serving overseas was undeniably difficult but absolutely fulfilling—because it was what God asked us to do.

Jesus engaged in many activities: miraculous healings, driving out demons, turning water into wine, debating with the Jewish leaders, having personal conversations with the lost, and even raising the dead! Imagine His popularity among the people as they realized His power. In Mark we find the disciples looking for Him because the crowds wanted Him to continue doing the amazing things He had done the night before. But listen to what Jesus said as He clarified why He came:

That evening after sunset the people brought to Jesus all the sick and demon-possessed. The whole town gathered at the door, and Jesus healed many who had various diseases. He also drove out many demons, but he would not let the demons speak because they knew who he was.

Very early in the morning, while it was still dark, Jesus got up, left the house and went off to a solitary place, where he prayed. Simon and his companions went to look for him, and when they found him, they exclaimed: "Everyone is looking for you!"

Jesus replied, "Let us go somewhere else—to the nearby villages—so I can preach there also. That is why I have come."

MARK 1:32-38, NIV

Jesus brought the Good News and was committed to preaching His eternal message—and to do it, He got involved with the people around Him. By healing and helping many as He walked among people, Jesus gained a following. During His brief ministry on earth, many people began to realize who He really was and why He came.

We need to pay attention to Jesus' intensity and intentionality as He spoke to, spent time with, and led His disciples. He knew that His parting commission to them would be to "go and make disciples." So as Jesus preached the good news, His disciples were always in the front-row seats. Throughout the gospels He gently led His disciples into situations that

He knew would prepare them for the task ahead. And Jesus did not avoid rebuke when it was necessary. His willingness to rebuke His disciples shows us that He valued them and desired that they would be men of character and godly response. And, above all, woven throughout His intentional relationship with them was His steadfast love for them.

Jesus modeled for us what it meant to be involved with people. His purposeful investment in the disciples was foundational to meeting the needs of the world. He preached the Kingdom, knowing that His disciples would take what He taught to the nations after He was gone.

CREATING AN ATMOSPHERE

A friend of mine always welcomes those she disciples into her living room. On her coffee table sits a candle and a beautiful tea service with delicate refreshments. This is how she communicates value to the women she meets with. It flows from her personal talents and heart. When she engages with women, she is truly a life-giver.

When I meet with women, the environment I cultivate doesn't look like my friend's. I am not like her—and that's okay! While the ambiance that I offer flows from my heart as well, I have met with women in restaurants, coffee shops, and office settings. I even met with someone in a rather plush bathroom at a high-end Nordstrom once! In the past few years I have really focused on inviting women into my home. Or—especially if they have little children—I go to their home. The home is a place where we are in charge of the noise and have opportunities to share deeply and pray inconspicuously.

Though location and physical setting are important, they are merely the concrete aspects within which the atmosphere flows. The key atmosphere choices we make are intangible yet crucial. And while many of these are unique to the different relationships, some are nonnegotiable. Every discipleship relationship should include five specific ingredients that will help ensure a life-giving atmosphere.

1. Confidentiality

Confidentiality means that we offer strict privacy for all that we share in conversation and life with someone. Confidentiality creates a safe environment. Now, some of us find a commitment to confidentiality easier than others do. I have been around women who have shared prayer requests that reveal the weaknesses of another woman. A friend once asked me to pray for someone who had shared something with her confidentially. We must not do this. Confidentiality is a privilege we carry. We have been entrusted with a precious piece of someone's heart, and we need to beware of telling others about her needs without her permission.

Never should a need, a weakness, a concern, or a fear of someone we disciple become a prayer request that we share with someone else. There is a word for when we do this: *gossip*! I say that with emphasis because it is so easy just to let things slip out.

I make this commitment of confidentiality to the women I meet with. Once, a young woman I was helping asked me a question that revealed some relational needs in her marriage. I later shared the question with a group of male ministry leaders because I thought they could help me answer it. But because of the details of the question, they could figure out who I was talking about. Even as I was "sharing" with these men, the Holy Spirit made me feel sick inside for speaking of this friend even though I did not mention her name. It was very difficult but absolutely necessary for me to let her know what I had done and ask for her forgiveness. She forgave me, but I could tell that she was cautious and reluctant in the conversations we had after that. There was a break in trust. And it was my fault.

Confidentiality creates trust and authentic exchange as we meet with those we disciple. When we fall short in this area, we need to quickly amend the broken trust.

2. Relationship

Have you ever considered that God created each of us with our own particular idiosyncrasies and wonders? What an amazing masterpiece each woman is! We each have different body shapes and sizes, voices, accents, interests, opinions, backgrounds, lifestyles, stories, problems, bosses, families, friends, children, husbands, talents, hopes, and dreams. Getting to know those we are discipling is like going on an adventure into the vast creative landscape and artistry of God.

The atmosphere at the heart of our discipling relationships should lean heavily toward being relational. We must view ourselves as coming alongside a friend, seeking to develop a rapport that produces mutual fondness and trust. As a wise man once told me, "We must build the bridge of relationship strong enough to bear the weight of truth." We are not ahead of those we disciple, nor are we behind them. Relationship affords us the opportunity to stand next to someone as we guide them forward.

Because we do share from the Scripture as we meet together, we need to keep the relational aspect of our connection front and center. We need to beware of falling into the mode of "I am the teacher and you are the student." Assuming the posture of teacher/student is especially easy and therefore a bit dangerous for those who have a gift of teaching, wisdom, or prophecy.

Seasons of life will color how we build relationships. In my earlier days I would often plan a get-together or a fun activity with those I was discipling. Usually during this season of life, we were the same age or just a few years apart. We did things that we both enjoyed, from shopping to going to the playground with our kids. Sometimes we might take a day trip together or go to a concert or play.

How we build relationships may change as seasons of life change. Other older women I know invite younger women over to cook or help in some home project. Some garden together. Others go on walks. While there are many ways to connect, I have found that when there is a vast age difference, we don't always have to "do something" to create trust and enjoyment in our relationship.

In the last two years I have been meeting with a young woman named Camille. I am in my sixties, and Camille is twenty-three! Camille meets regularly with and disciples college women. But from the outset of our commitment to meet together I let her know that I would not be "hanging out" with her the way she hangs out with the women she disciples. Instead, I wanted to hear about her life, her relationships, her worries, her future—I would not hold back, and I would be asking questions in a somewhat "maternal" way, if need be. Letting her know I was not going to try to act twenty-three years old was important for both of us. When she realized that "grandma" deeply cares about her but is not going to party with her, we both laughed—and I do believe I heard her sigh with relief! These days my hope is to share hearts with younger women conversationally as they tell me all about what they have faced or experienced.

Another important piece of building relationships? Laughing together! Laughing together produces a natural path to openness. The discipling relationship has a way of touching our scary, vulnerable spots. Being able to laugh together amid shared vulnerability creates an important emotional connection.

Emphasizing relationship is crucial for discipling. A genuine relationship frees us to share whatever we need to with the assurance of acceptance, care, and love.

3. Affirmation

Affirmation is not flattery. Flattery is defined as excessive or insincere praise. Flattery is a kind of inflated truth and can easily be manipulative. Compliments are also different from affirmation. Compliments tend to offer homage or applause to someone. That is okay. We do want to call out that which a person is good at. But compliments also can have a manipulative aspect and can be superfluous or even distracting from the deeper aspects of a person's heart and character.

Affirmation involves the assertion that something is true. Affirmation is a solid assessment offered to someone that speaks to character and growth. Affirmation speaks to what God is doing in and through a person. Listening to someone attentively as they share their heart affirms their value. We can affirm someone even as we pray for and bless them.

These questions can help us as we seek to affirm those we disciple:

- What is true and good about this woman?
- What is God doing "in her" that is wonderful?
- How is she responding in truth to Christ as He leads her down a difficult path?
- What aspect of her character that reflects kindness, godliness, or compassion might I commend?

Pay attention to her spiritual progress as you hear her share about her life. Asking good questions is an indispensable skill that invites those we disciple to analyze and investigate their responses and issues. Share your life experience when it is in sync with her experience or need, but for the most part let her do the talking. Listening to and hearing someone's heart is a form of affirmation. And we don't always have to have an answer. In fact, not having the answer is good because we can always pray with and for her. Trusting God alongside those we help models dependency upon Him.

Including affirmation in our discipling atmosphere helps us to build another up, always offering grace and truth in the words we share.

4. Intentionality

Intentionality simply means that we engage in forethought and deliberate planning before acting. Jesus lived this way and taught this way with the twelve disciples over the three years He was in ministry (Mark 1:38). Even the word *disciple* contains the seeds for intentionality. A disciple is one who follows and learns. As we help someone follow Christ, we offer them opportunity for learning through prepared scriptural content. Remember—at the root of this content is the aim of their attachment to Jesus. It is so easy to fall into the habit of teaching knowledge for knowledge's sake. Certainly knowledge will be passed on, but knowledge without wisdom can be dangerous!

To be intentional as we disciple merely means that we are responsibly thinking through what, how, and when we will share with those we meet with. It means that we offer structure with purpose for their growth. Have you ever attended a Zumba class where the instructor is not prepared? Without the intense, continuous Latin movement, the hour seems slow and wasted. Just like I appreciate a well-planned total dance workout from my Zumba instructor, so those we disciple deserve concerted attention to their growth needs.

You may ask at this point, "How can we be intentional and build relationship all at the same time?" Perhaps the words of Linnette, a young mom who actively disciples, will help: "I want to build a strong friendship with her. I also want to have a vision for the direction of our time spent together. As a disciplemaker, it is my job to prepare and plan for both friendship and vision during our time together."[17]

Because I tend to be a more spontaneous person, I often struggle with the concepts of structuring time and planning content. It is so much easier for me to flow freely without preparation. I fall into this frequently, so I write this because I know this is what is best—even if I must work at it even after years of discipling. Ultimately, I do the work of preparation because it is best for those I am discipling (not because I get a kick out of it!).

5. Love

True love in a healthy discipleship relationship has a couple different facets. First of all, love often includes exhortation. We live in an age where "love" is excessively tolerant. We are wary of saying anything that would deflate someone's self-image.

When Jesus expressed love, He always spoke that which was most constructive for that person in the long run. He seemed to refrain from saying anything that would give someone a false sense of security (see Mark 10:21). God is committed to the truth—*about us* and *for us*—because He loves us!

Exhortation is not only a spiritual gift but also a requirement for all believers (see Hebrews 10:25). *Exhortation* means to convey urgent advice or recommendations. It is a combination of counsel and warning combined with a sense of caution. There is also a place for rebuke should there be a need. Rebuke is stronger than exhortation and involves a stern talk or reprimand.

I bring up exhortation and rebuke here because we might need to help someone who wants to remain in her identity as a "victim" in life—someone who tends to wallow in her self-pity, remain angry, or continue in any other unhelpful attitude or actions. But *how* we confront someone is so vital. Sometimes we will need to be straightforward and share what we have observed. Hopefully she will be open to our advice because our "relationship is strong enough to bear the weight of the truth."

When I was in my twenties, the woman who discipled me told me that she was praying a certain verse over my life. The essence of this verse? That God would grow me from being a depressed personality to one who delights in Him. Her exhortation, though necessary and helpful, was hard to hear—but I paid attention. Indeed, I was often depressed, and my depression tended to "hang over" my life and conversations with others. Our brief conversation about that verse and her continued supportive prayer set me on a path of transformation and trust that changed me forever!

Just so you know—I had told her early in our discipling relationship that I wanted her to speak into my life, no matter what. And she did, but not too often. My fragile little personality would have been shattered! We need to be sensitive as we observe weaknesses in those we are helping. When we determine that we need to share something, we would be wise to first ask permission, regardless of a past agreement. And when we do take it upon ourselves to lovingly exhort or rebuke, we can purpose to avoid being blunt, abrasive, or condescending. Amy Carmichael calls us to consider our motivation if we need to rebuke: "If I can rebuke without a pang, then I know nothing of Calvary love."[18] Exhortation for those we are discipling will be necessary. Let us do so only because we long for the eventual joy that will result as they experience growth in Christ.

The second facet of love is that it needs to be unconditional. Unconditional love is absolute, total, and genuine. Because we are completely accepted by God, we must willingly accept others. Many broken people around us fear rejection. When we seek to truly love those around us, they need to know that there is nothing that they can do or say that will cause us to reject them. Communicating this kind of love creates an atmosphere that is safe and energized for mutual sharing.

When we love unconditionally we are not saying we applaud or agree with sinful or selfish behavior. But we are saying that no matter what, we have their back!

For my internship as a major in elementary education, I was assigned to a fifth-grade class in Bradenton, Florida. The teacher I was placed with was an older woman who was not "cool" by the world's standards. She was very strict with her class and smiled infrequently, but I noticed that her students loved and respected her.

The contrast between her class and the class of the new, young teacher down the hall was quite dramatic. The new teacher's class was loud, abrupt, and undisciplined. How they ever got any work done, I will never know! When I asked Mrs. Noon why her class was so orderly and responsive, she told me her secret: "My motto, Dana, is 'Be kind, but firm!'" Mrs. Noon taught me that there is a place for disciplinary expectations as we present a posture of warm acceptance. As we disciple, let's not be fooled by the voices around us that would oppose creating a positive structure from which sincere kindness flows.

If I were going to choose a passage that summarizes the atmosphere I long to create for the women I meet with, it would be Romans 12:9-18. As you read this passage, underline words that speak to your heart about creating the "right" atmosphere for discipling.

> Love must be honest and true. Hate what is evil.
> Hold on to what is good. Love one another deeply.
> Honor others more than yourselves. Stay excited
> about your faith as you serve the Lord. When you
> hope, be joyful. When you suffer, be patient. When

you pray, be faithful. Share with the Lord's people who are in need. Welcome others into your homes.

Bless those who hurt you. Bless them, and do not curse them. Be joyful with those who are joyful. Be sad with those who are sad. Agree with one another. Don't be proud. Be willing to be a friend of people who aren't considered important. Don't think that you are better than others.

Don't pay back evil with evil. Be careful to do what everyone thinks is right. If possible, live in peace with everyone. Do that as much as you can.

GO DEEPER

In his time with the Thessalonians, the apostle Paul was brimming with ways of relating that reflect much thought and experience on his part. Read through 1 Thessalonians 2:3-13 in your favorite translation, then answer the questions in your journal. Drink in the atmosphere that Paul sustained as he labored among the Thessalonians, and think about how Paul's ideas might help you create your atmosphere as you disciple women.

Verses 3-4

1. What were Paul's motives, purpose, and sense of calling as he shared the gospel with the audience in Thessalonica?
2. What three elements did *not* exist in his appeal, according to verse 3?

3. How did Paul view himself?

4. What actions and perspectives might we take if we seek only to please people as we disciple women?

Verses 5-6

5. Why do you think Paul was careful about offering any praise that might be considered flattery to the people to whom he ministered?

6. What is the difference between flattery and sincere praise?

7. Why was it important for Paul not to seek praise from those he ministered to?

8. As we disciple women, why is it important that we neither offer false praise nor seek praise?

9. How will this approach to praise create trust in our discipling relationships?

Verses 7-8

10. While he could have played the "authoritative apostle card," Paul was gentle among them like a mother caring for her little children. How does this image of a nurturing Paul influence your ideas about building a safe environment for discipleship?

11. How might our commitment to love well color the atmosphere we seek as we help others grow?

12. Think again of the picture of a mother caring gently for her little children. How are the principles of avoiding flattery, not letting people dodge potentially painful growth, and teaching the Word intrinsic to this picture?

Verses 9-10

13. Paul purposed not to burden the Thessalonians while he was with them. In what ways could we possibly burden those we are discipling?

14. Why is it important that we live holy and blameless lives as we engage in relationship with those we help?

15. How is living blamelessly different from purporting that we are perfect?

Verses 11-12

16. Paul also described himself as a father among the Thessalonians. How might Paul have been like a father as he connected to this community?

17. What characteristics of a father should we seek to bring to the environment of discipling?

Verse 13

18. What was Paul especially thankful for, and why do you think he emphasized this?

19. Paul "never stop[ped] thanking God," and he prayed for those he helped. In what ways can we integrate prayer into the climate we create for those we disciple?

20. Paul affirmed that the Thessalonians accepted the Word of God as from God not men. Why do you think he pointed this out to them?

21. Paul wrote, "[The Word of God] is really at work in you who believe." Why do we need to keep this truth central in our discipling context?

Review the full passage. List four conclusions you have reached as you consider generating a compelling environment for discipling:

I. _____

_____

_____

2. _____
   _____
   _____

3. _____
   _____
   _____

4. _____
   _____
   _____

YOUR DISCIPLING ATMOSPHERE

Whenever I read that passage from 1 Thessalonians I am always excited . . . and a bit overwhelmed. Paul set out a very high standard for us. The environment Paul put forth was one of transparent, genuine care in the context of teaching, challenge, and honesty.

After reading through the five vital elements of the discipling atmosphere listed earlier and delving into Paul's experience among the Thessalonians, perhaps you have some ideas about the discipling atmosphere you hope to create. Consider these questions to help you flesh out your ideas:

1. What impact do you think atmosphere has on the discipling relationship?

2. What fears, if any, do you have as you contemplate creating the right atmosphere?

3. Have you ever been in a relationship that was toxic or hurtful? Why was this atmosphere difficult for you? What ingredients made it toxic?

4. What have you learned from relationships that stimulated your growth?

5. As you imagine discipling someone who is close to your age, what fun things might you do so you can get to know each other?

6. How have you built relationships with others in your life?

7. Suppose you have no common interests with someone. How would you build a relationship in that situation?

8. What aspects of Paul's model do you want to provide through the atmosphere you create?

9. Which of the five ingredients will you emphasize? Which do you think will be difficult for you? How might you intentionally address those difficulties?

10. Record the elements that you feel are vital for you as you cultivate atmosphere.

DISCIPLEMAKER CHALLENGE

- Why do you think atmosphere is so valuable in the discipling relationship?

- How do you think ignoring the idea of atmosphere would affect your relationship with the one you want to disciple?

CHAPTER SIX

Whom Do We Help?

One day Jesus was walking beside the Sea of Galilee. There he saw two brothers, Simon Peter and his brother Andrew. They were throwing a net into the lake, because they were fishermen. "Come and follow me," Jesus said. "I will send you out to fish for people." At once they left their nets and followed him. ❧ MATTHEW 4:18-20

The things you have heard me say in the presence of many witnesses entrust to reliable people who will also be qualified to teach others.
❧ 2 TIMOTHY 2:2, NIV

SANDRA WAS TWENTY-TWO and a new college graduate. During her time in college she had been active in a campus ministry, but she had not been discipled. Her desire to grow and walk with God oozed from her heart, smile, and words.

At the same time, I had been praying that God would bring me a young woman in her twenties whom I could disciple. I wanted to connect with a hungry young woman who would challenge my walk with God.

Sandra emailed me one day and asked if we could talk

about discipling. When we met to talk, I was pretty sure she was an answer to my prayer, but I didn't want to assume that. As we chatted about being a disciple and discipling others, her enthusiasm and attentiveness drew me in. We both agreed to pray over our relationship, asking God to show us if we should meet together.

If we have asked God to bring us someone He wants us to disciple, we need to be on the lookout! The question of who we help can feel a bit daunting, but be encouraged: there is a kind of spiritual logic that leads us toward those whom God would have us help.

In this chapter we will work together to identify where we might find women to disciple and what basic qualities we hope to catch sight of in those we might disciple.

As we examine this question—"Whom do we help?"— don't panic! As we consider whom we might disciple, God is more concerned about a fruitful outcome than we are, and He will walk with us.

GOD DOES THE CHOOSING

When I first began discipling, I often felt overwhelmed when trying to find someone to help. I wondered if anyone would ever want to meet with me! But God helped me to see that I needed to trust Him at every moment in this adventure of discipling women.

John 15:16 brought calm to my spirit, and I rest in it to this day when it comes to discipling women:

You did not choose me. Instead, I chose you.
I appointed you so that you might go and bear fruit
that will last. [The Father] will give you whatever
you ask for in my name.

This verse is pregnant with promise for us, and it hints at a general rule we can adopt as we wonder who we should help:

Pray, watch, and receive!

Whether we are seasoned or novice disciplers, we can rest in the fact that God has not only asked us to make disciples but also chosen us to help other women grow. By faith we pray, we watch, and we receive those women God sends our way.

We can also take confidence in the fact that the journey of discipleship for each individual woman does not rest on our shoulders alone. As I think about the various women I have met with over the years, I realize that I am but one link in the chain of their process toward maturity.

God usually brings two people together in a discipling relationship for a particular season. What happens is this: I am present and in the same location as a certain woman. I am praying that God will show me someone He wants me to meet with. I begin to "see" her. She grows aware of her need for growth. God leads us to meet together. We agree upon why and for what aspect of her growth God has brought us together. Then after a season of meeting together, we naturally transition away from the relationship as we move to different locations or arenas of life.

People come and people go in our lives. We move, they move. And as we walk out our own journey, we are privileged to have the opportunity to invest in a few as we go. Pray, watch, receive!

Now this is not to say that impermanence is always the case. One woman I know has met with certain women from the day they came to Christ until now. She continues to be a friend, coach, and mentor to them. Another friend of mine established a woman as a disciple and continued to meet with her until she was an active, fruitful disciplemaker. So though in my life I have moved often and invested in a rather patchy way, many have been used in this durable, continual way! We must not compare ourselves with others as we trust God to use our life as a disciplemaker—it will look different for each of us (see 2 Corinthians 10:12).

Though God does the choosing and has uniquely crafted each of us as a discipler, when it comes to discerning who He wishes us to help, we as disciplers must cultivate and rely on the crucial quality of *being present*. *Being present* means paying profound attention to the moment we are in. Without this quality, we find ourselves unduly concentrating on an unrelated task or distraction instead of focusing on the people around us.

If we want to truly recognize those God sends our way, we need to be present in the various settings of our lives—meetings, parties, work, community events, church. It is possible to pass through any of these events without being present. If we aren't present, we might miss God showing us the one we are praying for, watching for, and ready to receive. And while we should be present in every aspect of life, there are four general ways I have noticed God tends to reveal the one He wishes me to disciple.

1. Right Under Our Noses

Early in my discipling journey, I found women to disciple through a couple's Bible study that Tom and I led while he was attending vet school at Purdue. I began meeting one-on-one with two of the wives in that study. This was easy and very natural. We liked each other. We already had personal relationships in full swing. I was just a year or two older than them, and a little further down the road in the mothering journey. I would often invite them to meet in my home during the children's naptime. Though I did share prepared scriptural content and earnestly sought to teach them, these friends later told me, "We really loved our time in the Word with you and all you passed on to us. But it was what we caught as we watched you raise your kids more than what you taught."

I had a similar experience with the woman who equipped me on the "how-to" of discipling women. She taught me that in discipling one-on-one I must always bring the "Word, prayer, and life" when I spend time with another in a natural yet intentional way. She invested in my life in these three ways. She and her husband were ten years older than Tom and me, and as we prayed together they modeled the wisdom that we knew we needed as we became parents. We were taught a lot, and we caught a lot.

Sometimes you don't have to look too far when you disciple someone—she could be someone who is already naturally integrated into your life, someone who is already looking to you for guidance and an example.

2. At Church

When we moved to a community in the Chicago area, God began to bring women who would ask me to disciple them. I was in my early thirties, nurturing toddlers at home, prepping to go overseas, and loving life. The women I met with during this season seemed to find me and ask me for help. I think this happened for two reasons. First, I began praying earnestly that God would send women to me whom I could help grow. Second, as we settled into our local church and served however we could, we came to know many different people. As I became involved in our church, God established my reputation as a "discipler."

When we take on the task of discipling one-on-one, we need to be engaged in a viable community that supports and promotes the vision and implementation of disciplemaking. The church across America provides wonderful communities for women. To be a part of such a community will ensure growth! Discipling women within the church's women's community means that we have natural connections that offer support and accountability.

We are all members of a greater community, and as disciplers we need to understand how we fit into the vision of our church congregation. Ideally, the pastor and women's director will advocate discipling through the church vision, from the pulpit, and among the weekly opportunities provided for women. As we disciple other women in our church we need to know that it is part of the vision of our church leadership. We need a framework that launches and supports us. Perhaps the leaders in our local church offer programs that include training and vision for disciplemaking. Imagine if every church had a continual flow of women (and men) who felt personally responsible to reach others for Christ, disciple all believers, and equip others to do the same!

3. Through Ministry Leaders

During our time overseas, I wanted to be involved with women on the campus where Tom was leading the ministry, but raising kids and living in a third-world culture were dramatically draining. Tom understood my desire to disciple women from our campus ministry so he conferred with our women's staff worker, Butet, and they helped to connect me with women on campus who wanted to be discipled. It relieved me to have Tom and Butet broker the way as they connected me with these young women.

For some of us, the women leaders in our church can assist us and broker the initial step as we set out to discern those whom we might disciple. These women leaders are most aware of those who are ready to be discipled. When you desire to disciple someone, set up an appointment with the women's director and begin the conversation about who might be available and ready to be discipled. Ask the women's director to meet with you once a month or every two months after you start discipling for review and advice. Seeking to find discipling relationships through the help of ministry leaders allows us to contribute in a vital way to what God is doing among the women in our church.

4. Through God's Prompting

Anna, a high school girl, showed great spunk in sharing her faith in God among non-believers at a public gathering. I saw her heart for God as she spoke before a large group of people. Her countenance drew me to her. Her spunk was not shrouded in pride but in a circumspect fashion as she engaged with others. I found myself attracted to her poignant resolve!

Since she was still in high school, I pursued meeting with her only after interacting with her parents, who supported the idea. Meeting with her has been not unlike a cross-cultural experience since we are almost five decades apart in age! I am thankful that she is open and hungry for God. As a woman of her generation, she holds the seeds to the future for the spreading of the gospel, and she is already listening to God about how she can take part in His global strategy. It is not rare that after meeting with Anna I find myself invigorated by her crisp enthusiasm for being a strong disciple of Jesus as well as her determination to share the gospel with everyone around her.

The wonderful thing about "God's promptings" is that they come along at the most unexpected places and times. If we can't get away from that inaudible voice of God's Spirit drawing us to a person's need for discipleship, we need to, at the least, pray the option through. Just be open to the Lord!

THE QUALITIES OF A DISCIPLE

God will be faithful to give us opportunities to help others. And when we study Scripture, we see that Jesus was purposeful and prayerful in His choice of the twelve disciples. Ultimately, He didn't just want the disciples to come to know Him and grow in Him—His goal was also that they might help others and ultimately fill the world with faithfulmembers of His family. As we pray, watch, and receive, we should look for certain qualities in those we might help.

1. **Heart for God:** Does this woman have a **heart** for God? Does she talk about her faith and how God is at work in her life and around her? Is she responsive to His leading, even if it is not easy? Does she appreciate and exhibit obedience to His Word? Does she acknowledge Christ's authority in her life?

2. **Hungry to grow:** Does this woman **responsibly perceive her need for growth**? Is she willing to mutually

defer as we uncover what God leads us to work through, as we share in prayer, and as we share our hearts? Have I seen her respond to other opportunities for growth?

3. **Available for help:** Will this woman make herself **available** according to the mutual commitment we have mapped out for the agreed-upon period of time? Will she flex her schedule for meeting if need be? Will she prioritize our discipling relationship at this time in her life?

4. **Heart for people:** Does this woman earnestly desire to **see others** around her come to know Christ and grow? Is she involved with people?

Other disciplers I know use the acronym **FAT** to help discern the qualities in someone they might disciple.

F: Is she **faithful** to God and those who want to help her grow?

A: Is she **available** when the opportunities to grow are placed in front of her?

T: Is she **teachable** as she gets into the Word and hears from God?

These characteristics are the raw material of a woman who wants to be discipled. In actuality, she is making a commitment to herself to grow, and she is aware that she needs help as she grows. As disciplers, we are there to assist her, come alongside her, and point her to what Jesus teaches and wants to do in her life. Above all, we as disciplers must be open to the leading of God, who will direct us to those with these qualities.

Several years ago I was *not* praying that God would give me an opportunity to invest in a woman one-on-one—and then He brought Jenna into my life. At the time I was serving on a national leadership team, traveling frequently, and taking care of our last child at home. I could not imagine adding one more thing to my busy schedule!

One day Jenna invited me to go on a walk. As we walked, she turned to me with exuberance and asked, "I know that you are super busy, but would you meet with me?" I told her she was exactly right—I was extremely busy. Rather begrudgingly I agreed to pray about her request, but I said that God probably would direct me to say no. Her face fell a little.

"But you will pray?" she asked.

As I prayed about Jenna, God kept bringing to my mind the caliber of young woman she was. She had a heart for God, was hungry to grow, was available whenever I was, and had a heart for people. He kept reminding me that she demonstrated all of the qualities we just went through, and that her enthusiasm for Christ and helping other women was amazing. Indeed, she was unusual. To be honest, I believe God wanted me to meet with her as much for my benefit as hers. This young woman's fervent concern for the things of God and the women around her absolutely revitalized me.

As we live life—in our neighborhoods, families, churches, and communities of friends—let's watch for God's leading toward women with these four qualities. Pray, watch, and receive!

========= *ello* =========

📖 GO DEEPER

Observing the life of Jesus Christ can help us as we pray about and determine who we might disciple. Since it was His idea to "go and make disciples" in the first place, we can be assured that He modeled all we need to understand as we step into discipling! Read through the Scripture in this section in your favorite translation, and answer the questions in your journal. Lean in to observe the life of Jesus as He speaks with, gets to know, and invites the original twelve disciples.

John 1:35-50

Verses 35-37

1. How do you think John the Baptist must have felt as he told his followers to go follow Jesus instead?

2. How do you think John's two followers felt?

3. Why was it important for John the Baptist to release his followers to Jesus?

4. What can we learn from John's example as we meet with those God gives us?

Verses 38-39

5. These verses describe three of Jesus' actions as He interacted with the two followers: (1) He turned around; (2) He saw them; and (3) He asked them. As you consider each of these actions, how does this inform your answer to the question "Whom do I help?"

6. Jesus asked the followers, "What do you want?" Why do you think He asked them this?

7. What does it look like, practically, when you "see" someone?

8. Do you think the two followers had a good answer? Why or why not?

9. If Jesus asked you, "What do you want?" what would be your answer?

10. What do you think Jesus had in mind when He invited them to "come and see"?

11. When we disciple others, what are we inviting them to "come and see"?

Verses 40-42

12. Why do you think Andrew went to get his brother, Simon?

13. What do we learn from Andrew's actions about finding those we might help?

14. What can we take away from this inspirational chat that Jesus had with Peter as we begin to connect with those we disciple?

Verses 43-46

15. What can we learn from Jesus as we watch Him "find" Philip, the one He wanted to help?

16. Philip went to find Nathanael. What do you learn about the question of who we help from Philip's actions?

Verses 47-50

17. Theologians are not sure if Nathanael was one of the twelve disciples. Some say he was the disciple also called Bartholomew. If he did not become one

of the twelve disciples, what can you learn from the connection Jesus made with him as He sought out disciples?

Luke 5:1-11

Verses 1-4

18. How do Jesus' actions illustrate the kind of relationship that He had with Peter at this point?

19. Why do you think Jesus directed Peter to let down his nets?

Verses 5-8

20. When asked to lower his nets in deeper water, Peter responded logically but still did as Jesus asked. What do Peter's obedient words and actions reveal about his heart?

21. Why do you think Peter was overwhelmed by his sin?

Verses 9-11

22. Why do you think Jesus told Peter not to be afraid just before telling him that from now on he would catch people?

23. As a result of this call, Peter and the others left their boats and everything else they had. How does their response answer the question of who we help?

Mark 3:13-19

Verses 13-15

24. Why do you think Jesus appointed only twelve men to be with Him? For what were these men appointed?

25. What significance might the number of disciples recruited by Jesus have for us as we think about helping women?

26. Jesus did not send the disciples to seminary or remove them from society

to teach them. He just took them "with Him." What does this help us to understand as we disciple someone?

Verses 16-19

27. Jesus immediately renamed Simon as Peter, which means "rock." Why do you think Jesus renamed Peter?

28. The final disciple listed is Judas Iscariot. How might the fact that Jesus recruited one who failed Him encourage us as disciplers?

29. What lessons do you take away from this passage as you consider who you might help?

DISCERNMENT

So who will *you* help? This is where the rubber meets the road in discipling. It places us in a vulnerable position. Consider the following questions and thoughts with honesty and humble reflection:

- What apprehensions do you feel as you consider praying for someone to help?

- List names of women God has placed in your life. Do you "see" anyone as you pray about and are present in the lives of these women?

- Develop a plan of action. Go talk to the woman God has helped you to see. Initiate with her. And if God leads, invite her to pray about being discipled. If you do not have a specific woman in mind, go and talk to your pastor or the women's director of your church. See if they have any suggestions regarding women you might pray about discipling.

Pray over the following passage as you pray for those God has put on your heart:

> The one who plants is not important. The one who waters is not important. It is God who makes things grow. He is the important one. The one who plants and the one who waters have the same purpose. The Lord will give each of them a reward for their work. We work together to serve God. You are like God's field. You are like his building.
> God has given me the grace to lay a foundation as a wise builder. Now someone else is building on it. But each one should build carefully. No one can lay any other foundation than what has already been laid. That foundation is Jesus Christ.
>
> 1 CORINTHIANS 3:7-11

This passage reminds us we cannot make someone grow—but God will! We work together with God. We are colaborers with Him, relying on His transforming grace as we build on the foundation of Jesus Christ. As we work together with God, we can be sure of the promise Christ gave us in Matthew 28:20: "You can be sure that I am always with you, to the very end."

📜 DISCIPLEMAKER CHALLENGE

- What might be the negative effects of making disciples within our churches without the support of the pastor and/or women's director?

- Why do you think it is crucial to fit in as part of your church's vision both relationally and organizationally?

CHAPTER SEVEN

What Do We Share?

By this time you ought to be teachers yourselves, yet here I find you need someone to sit down with you and go over the basics on God again, starting from square one—baby's milk, when you should have been on solid food long ago! Milk is for beginners, inexperienced in God's ways; solid food is for the mature, who have some practice in telling right from wrong. ❧ HEBREWS 5:12-14, MSG

I have shown you to the disciples you gave me out of the world. They were yours. You gave them to me. And they have obeyed your word. Now they know that everything you have given me comes from you. I gave them the words you gave me. And they accepted them. They knew for certain that I came from you. They believed that you sent me. I pray for them. I am not praying for the world. I am praying for those you have given me, because they are yours. ❧ JOHN 17:6-9

FIRSTBORN CHILDREN TEND to suffer the hassle of crazed parents who are basically in test mode as they seek to wisely raise their child. I don't know how many times we have apologized to our first child, Michael, for all the mistakes we made "on him"! We were determined and unrelenting as we applied all that we had stored up for our innocent little one. Only in hindsight

THE GENTLE ART OF DISCIPLING WOMEN

did we realize that it was our other children who benefited from everything we required our firstborn to endure.

When we start out as parents, we have to entertain a lot of questions and sort through countless ideas about how to raise a child. One basic question that every parent faces is, "What should I feed my baby?" Regardless of whether we want to breastfeed or use formula, I think we can all agree that milk of some sort is what every baby should start with! Certainly we would never cram grilled salmon down our new baby's throat, no matter how convinced we are of its nutritional value. And we can likewise agree that we would not continue to give only milk to our two-year-old. The food we offer babies and children should reflect their physical development as well as what is best and necessary for their nutritional health.

When we think of feeding our babies, we probably look through the latest scientific research about what foods we should feed them, when we should feed them these foods, and when we should move to the next phase of foods. As we seek to feed our children wisely, we also have a major goal in mind—that every child we nourish would one day be able to sit at the big-people table and feed themselves!

This next key discipleship question, "What do we share?" requires us to act as a new mother researching how best to feed her child. We need to pray over the woman we're discipling and ask God to reveal where this woman is in her growth journey so that we may best discern what we should share in our time with her. Scripture supports the idea that as believers we each experience a spiritual journey that began even before we were born:

Lord, you have seen what is in my heart.
> You know all about me.
You know when I sit down and when I get up.
> You know what I'm thinking even though you are far
> > away.
You know when I go out to work and when I come back
> home.
> You know exactly how I live.
Lord, even before I speak a word,
> you know all about it. . . .

None of my bones was hidden from you
> when you made me inside my mother's body.
> That place was as dark as the deepest parts of the
> > earth.
When you were putting me together there,
> your eyes saw my body even before it was formed.
You planned how many days I would live.
> You wrote down the number of them in your book
> before I had lived through even one of them.

PSALM 139:1-4, 15-16

THE PATH TO MATURITY

But where to begin? How can we truly start discerning where a woman is in her growth in Christ so that we may best help her?

Each believer experiences several phases of growth on

the path to maturity. Understanding our own journey will help us to empathize and realize the needs of others. And knowing the phases of growth helps us discover what help a woman needs and therefore, ultimately, what we should share with her. I call the path to maturity the B Process:

The B Process

2 CORINTHIANS 5:17-18

BEFORE

*Your eyes saw my body even **before** it was formed. You planned how many days I would live. You wrote down the number of them in your book **before** I had lived through even one of them.*
PSALM 139:16

BELIEVE

*Being right with God does not come from my obeying the law. It comes because I **believe** in Christ. It comes from God because of faith.*
PHILIPPIANS 3:9

BELONG

*We are God's creation. He created us to **belong** to Christ Jesus.*
EPHESIANS 2:10

Give praise to the God and Father of our Lord Jesus Christ. He has blessed us with every spiritual blessing.

Those blessings come from the heavenly world.
*They belong to us because we **belong** to Christ.*
EPHESIANS 1:3

BECOME

*God **began** a good work in you. And I am sure that he **will***
***carry it on** until it is completed.*
PHILIPPIANS 1:6

BUILD OTHERS

He brought us back to himself through Christ's death on the
*cross. And he has given us the task of **bringing others** back to*
him through Christ.
2 CORINTHIANS 5:18

We work together to serve God. You are like God's field.
You are like his building. God has given me the grace to lay
*a foundation as **a wise builder**.*
Now someone else is building on it.
1 CORINTHIANS 3:9-10

To understand the depth and the breadth of God's love and forgiveness in our lives, we first must reflect on our journey **before** Christ. This story begins in our childhood. For some, this story is full of brokenness, fear, and deep needs. For others, this story starts in a solid Christian home where they do not remember a time when they were not hearing about Christ.

Those who come from an abyss of woundedness often find it easy to describe their transition to faith. Those who grew up in a Christian environment with Christian activity at every turn might find it more difficult to pinpoint where the story of their personal faith started. But no matter our story, all of us at some time in our lives turned from trusting something other than Christ to completely relying upon Him. This is our **believe** story. Looking back and identifying what it was about Jesus and ourselves that brought us to a place of trusting helps us when we want to help others.

At some point after initially trusting Christ we step into and begin to own our identity in Christ. We begin to comprehend that we **belong** to Him and are now members of His royal family. As our identity is increasingly anchored in Christ, there is a shift forward as we step into **becoming** all that Christ has for us. This process of becoming, as we discussed in chapter 4, is pledged to every believer as the Holy Spirit draws them forward. Jesus promises to "make everything new" the moment we entrust our hearts and lives to Him. Belonging (identity in Christ) and becoming are intertwined and can occur simultaneously. We are all in God's process of becoming throughout our lifetime.

As we make every effort to become all God has designed us to be, He shows us that there is work to be done! Just as others have helped us to grow, now we can begin to invest in and build others. As Elisabeth Elliot so wisely shared, "Maturity starts with the willingness to give oneself."[19] God draws us into His heart for the world and gives us the privilege of colaboring with Him by bringing others to Christ and

building them up as laborers. Discipling is part of the skill set integral to building others.

Most of the women we will disciple will be new believers stepping into their newfound identity of belonging to Christ or into the stage of becoming. We can let them tell us where they feel they are along their path to maturity. Questions to help them reflect on this might include

- What was your life like before you came to know Christ?
- What attracted you to Christ?
- What relief or changes occurred for you when you came to Christ?
- What struggles did you have or do you have as a believer?
- Have you had women around you who were models of faith either before or after you believed?
- How does the truth that you now belong to Jesus help you in your life?
- When disappointments come or relational conflicts occur, how does belonging to Jesus help you through?
- How strong are you in the Word?
- Do you have a daily time in the Word and prayer?
- Share how you have been growing in the last year. What topics, experiences, and lessons stand out to you?

- What studies in the Word have helped you grow or changed your life? Why?
- Where on the B Process would you place yourself? Where would you like to be? How will you get there?

After you have generally discerned where a woman is in her path to maturity in Christ, you can consider content that you might delve into in the days ahead. We all know that it is God's desire that every believer would fully mature in Christ. As disciplers, it is our obligation to ensure that those we help receive teaching and assistance that boosts them toward maturity (see Colossians 1:28-29).

GUIDELINES FOR SHARING

As we disciple women, there are several guidelines we can adhere to as we pray about and plan for their spiritual diet. If we do not pay attention to these guidelines, we will be frustrated—and so will the women we disciple.

1. Begin with the End in Mind

The end game for the new believer is maturity in Christ. Ultimately we want them to strongly attach to Jesus through His Word and prayer. We want them to be mature in their walk; dependent upon the Holy Spirit; and fluent in hearing, understanding, and obeying God's voice. We want them to daily step off into life from a strong foundation of connection with Jesus. And the pinnacle of anyone's maturity is the heart to help others know and grow in Christ—that is, to disciple others!

Knowing where she came from spiritually, where she is now, and where she needs to go in the next six months of her life provides the framework for content selection. Does she need reinforcements of the "pure milk of the Word"? Is she ready to take on solid food and grow stronger in her faith? Or is she noticing the needs of others' growth around her and needing to be equipped to help others grow? Preparing content with the end in mind will give healthy momentum to the time we spend together.

2. Share the Word

The primary responsibility we have as disciplers is to always teach and share the Word with those we are helping. Jesus said, "Heaven and earth will pass away. But my words will never pass away" (Matthew 24:35). It is so easy in our world today to spend time talking about anything and everything but His Word. But we need to look at the example of Jesus. When tempted by Satan in Matthew 4, Jesus combated the devil with the Scripture, and He was not thrown off when the devil wrongly quoted Scripture back at Him in an attempt to manipulate Him. Jesus told the devil,

> Man shall not live and be upheld and sustained by bread alone, but by every word that comes forth from the mouth of God.
>
> MATTHEW 4:4, AMP

In Indonesia they have a saying: "Kalau tidak makan nasi, tidak makan!" This means, "If you haven't eaten rice, you haven't eaten!" Similarly, if we have not shared the Word, we have not truly discipled! Not delving into the Word with those we are discipling is akin to meeting with them for a meal and giving them an empty plate. To be faithful as we disciple someone, we must always share His Word.

3. Don't Assume Anything

One of my personal weaknesses as I have met one-on-one with women over the years is that I often assume a woman is more mature than she truly is. It is easy to distort a woman's spiritual needs—especially if, for example, she has a doctorate degree, her dad is a pastor, or she has gone to church her whole life. It takes great humility on the part of both the discipler and the one she is helping to gear up and go after the basics of the Christian life. In the past few years I have learned that when I help someone who is between eighteen and twenty-five, I don't care what their background is: they need the basics!

Without the pure milk of the Word in a person's life, they get malnourished. Hebrews 5 clues us into the deficits those believers will suffer because they never grow up in their faith. They will not grow to the healthy place where they are ready and able to teach others (v. 12), and they will miss out on living the joyous, godly life God desires for them (vv. 13-14). I wonder how many "Peter Pan believers" fly among us!

4. Remember to Keep It Simple

It is not uncommon to overthink what we need to share. Sometimes we think we have to make discipling equivalent to getting a higher degree! Remember: the first disciplers included fishermen, tax collectors, and even a murderer. Listen to what was said about them:

> When they saw the courage of Peter and John and realized that they were unschooled, ordinary men, they were astonished and they took note that these men had been with Jesus.
>
> ACTS 4:13, NIV

As we seek to disciple women, the most important thing is not that we have been to seminary or read every book we can find on discipleship. Rather, it is that we know and have been with Jesus. Because we know Him, we can share Him. We can keep our prep simple. Discussing, sharing, and praying over one or two foundational verses with a woman is much more valuable than presenting her with the top ten things we know about some complicated and controversial topic.

Even when someone is fairly mature, we need to humbly and simply prepare from the Word for them. Keeping it simple makes it applicable and doable for us, the disciplers!

Later on in this chapter, we'll get into some details about how to prepare specific content. The hope is that eventually you will prepare content out of the wealth of your depth in the Word and life experiences—but let's say that someone has asked you to disciple them and you want to start straight away. Lack of prepared content should never be a reason not to disciple! Rather, I would recommend two quick and easy options that will lead to tremendous discussion and will deepen your relationship with each other.

The first and very natural option would be to use the first four chapters of this book. Take your time as you go through them with the woman you're discipling. The first four chapters could take eight meetings and be very beneficial. As you walk through the four foundational topics for authentic faith, share your life and perspective honestly as you answer the questions. Seek to encourage the woman you're discipling as she shares, and gently challenge her as you observe areas of growth that she needs.

Or, second, go through a book of the Bible together. I have done this many times. I would recommend choosing from three books of the Bible in particular. First, I would consider the book of John. A woman who is fairly new to Christ and the church would benefit greatly from reading the book of John with you. Simply read one to three chapters each time you meet, asking her what stands out to her and discussing what seems relevant to her growth. There are twenty-one chapters in John, so three chapters per meeting would provide content for seven meetings.

If the woman asking me to disciple her is more aware of the Word, I might choose either the book of Colossians or Philippians. These two books point the disciple to depth and understanding of the Christian life. Mainly, as you get together make sure you are in the Word together, sharing your hearts and praying each time!

📖 GO DEEPER

Before we step into the actual content we might develop and share as we disciple, let's turn to and study what Jesus did, prayed for, and taught His disciples. John 17 shows us the heart of Jesus as the Master Disciplemaker. At this point in time Jesus was suffering immensely because He was about to go to the cross. He knew He would be leaving the disciples. What He prayed about in John 17 gives us insight into what topics He prioritized as He spent time with His disciples. As you read through John 17:6-20 in your favorite translation and answer the questions in your journal, seek to detect what Jesus "shared" with His disciples.

Verses 6-8

1. What is the first thing Jesus said He showed His disciples? Where did His disciples come from?
2. What did Jesus relate about God's Word here? What is the difference between accepting God's Word and obeying His Word?
3. How do you think emphasizing God's Word to His disciples proved Christ's origins to them?
4. How do we show the Father to those we disciple?
5. Where do women we help come from?
6. How important is the Scripture as we disciple?

Verses 9-10

7. If His disciples belong to His Father, why do you think Jesus prayed for them?

8. How do you think glory came to Jesus through His disciples?

9. Why should we pray for those we disciple? Why should we teach them to pray?

10. How do you think your life as a discipler brings glory to Jesus?

11. How might those you disciple bring glory to Jesus?

Verses 11-12

12. Jesus emphasized the safety of His disciples. What concerns do you think He had for them?

13. How do we guard those we disciple? What are we protecting them from?

14. What influences of the world do we combat as we seek to help others know Christ?

15. What influences distract those around you from walking deeply with Christ?

16. How can we share this with those we disciple?

Verse 13

17. Why do you think Jesus longs for His followers to know joy?

18. Why is joy an important aspect of following Christ?

19. How can we share or teach about joy?

Verse 14

20. Jesus stated that He has given His disciples God's Word. Why do you think the Word is so central in all that Jesus mentions in this prayer?

21. What place should Scripture have as we disciple women?

Verses 15-16

22. Jesus realized the tension that we and those we disciple will face as we live

in the world though we are not "of the world." What tensions do you face as you live in the world? What tensions do those you disciple face?

Verses 17-19

23. Jesus prayed that His disciples might be sanctified or "made holy." He also said that His disciples have been sent in to the world. Why is it important that those who are sent see the value in being made holy?

24. How are we both *made* perfect (complete) and *being made* holy (in process)?

25. What do we share with those we disciple when it comes to living a holy life? Why is this important for each of us?

Verse 20

26. Jesus modeled praying for His disciples throughout this prayer. He was also praying for us and those we disciple in this final request. How does this generational aspect of His prayer make you feel both as His disciple and as one who disciples others?

27. How important is it that we pray for those we disciple?

28. How important is it that we teach them about prayer?

29. Read through John 17 again. How do you think Jesus would answer our question, "What do we share?"

DISCERNING WHAT TO SHARE

Now that we have set the foundation for how to approach someone's growth, it is time for us to think through what we would share in a one-on-one discipling relationship. To help us, let's examine how Peter and the author of Hebrews described the content they shared as they went from town to town and spent time with people.

Peter was very clear that new believers need to be given

what he called the "pure milk of God's word" (1 Peter 2:2). Paul complemented what Peter taught by delineating levels of input. He urged the Corinthian believers to grow in a healthy manner. He was frustrated because he was hoping they could handle input that he described as "solid food," but he ended up admonishing them for not yet taking in and applying the basic teachings of "milk":

> Brothers and sisters, I couldn't speak to you as people who live by the Holy Spirit. I had to speak to you as people who were still following the ways of the world. You aren't growing as Christ wants you to. You are still like babies. The words I spoke to you were like milk, not like solid food. You weren't ready for solid food yet. And you still aren't ready for it.
>
> 1 CORINTHIANS 3:1-2

In the book of Hebrews we find the author also distinguishing between the basics of "the pure milk" of the Word and the "solid food" teaching that deepens maturity. But then he moved beyond that, sharing the hope that we eventually would be able to teach others:

> We have a lot to say about this. But it is hard to make it clear to you. That's because you are no longer trying to understand. By this time you should be teachers. But in fact, you need someone to teach you all over again. You need even the simple truths

of God's word. You need milk, not solid food.
Anyone who lives on milk is still a baby. That person
does not want to learn about living a godly life.
Solid food is for those who are grown up. They have
trained themselves to tell the difference between
good and evil. That shows they have grown up.

HEBREWS 5:11-14

Content for those who are being equipped to teach
others requires that they should partake of a more refined
"solid food," which we might, for purposes of clarity, call
"meat."

I love that these categories are based in Scripture and
compared to food. We all understand not only the need
for food, but the need of it to be prepped and offered
progressively in the life of a child. Let's dig a little deeper
into each of these spiritual food groups: milk, solid food,
and meat.

Milk

Peter and the author of Hebrews emphasized the need for
starting growth with the basic teachings of the Word. As
we think of the "pure milk" of the Word, we need to ensure
that those we help have a strong foundation in their understanding of Scripture. Sometimes we can bypass basic qualities of God's Word—like the inspiration or essentiality of
the Word—because we assume others just know this! When

we think about the women we are helping to grow, we must assess the following:

- Does she understand that God's Word is inspired, vitally important, and compulsory for our growth?
- Does she long for the Scriptures and make the choice to be in His Word daily?
- When relational or circumstantial difficulties arise, does she immediately run to Jesus and rest upon His Word? Or does she spiral downward in an emotional reaction?

Sustainable growth is founded upon Christ and His Word. Even in the Old Testament we find Moses emphasizing the importance of God's Word:

> Think carefully about all of the words I have announced to you today. I want you to command your children to be careful to obey all of the words of this law. They aren't just useless words for you. *They are your very life.* If you obey them, you will live in the land for a long time.
> DEUTERONOMY 32:46-47, EMPHASIS ADDED

Like Moses we want to ensure that those we help realize that life springs up out of a deep, abiding connection to God through His Word. If the woman you are discipling does not have a personal, private life flowing out of time spent with Jesus in the Word, make sure that you intentionally emphasize meeting Jesus daily in His Word. Just like a baby needs milk, the disciple needs the Word for healthy growth toward maturity. If we are not attaching to Jesus through daily interaction with Him in His Word, many other voices and ideas will vie for our allegiance.

My friend Karla began spending time with Wendy, a young woman who had recently come to Christ. As they built their discipling relationship, Karla began noticing that many things were drawing Wendy's attention away from the wisdom of the Scriptures: books like *The Secret*, which offers some interesting but futile advice on approaching our life path; talk show hosts offering to lead her down the self-help enlightened road; and the conventional advice subtly taught through the lens of our culture and media.

Karla realized that Wendy had been not only paying attention to these philosophies but also making some life choices rooted in these ideas. There was no evidence that Wendy was going to the Word for life guidance, and her choices were indeed leading her down a self-destructive path. As they chatted about these alluring ideas, the Holy Spirit led my friend Karla to share a thought from the Word she had meditated on during her quiet time that morning: "What good is it if someone gains the whole world but loses their soul?" (Matthew 16:26).

Karla genuinely modeled valuing the Word as she shared this bit of "milk" with Wendy. Wendy, so new to her walk with Christ, immediately drank in the meaning of the verse.

Her eyes filled with tears as the Holy Spirit translated the Word into her life.

Many do not realize the supernatural qualities of a life in Christ and His Word. So we need to seriously consider how those we help view the Scriptures and whether they are living from Scripture. But before we can help another woman become strong in the Scriptures, we must examine ourselves:

- How did I become rooted in Scripture?
- What world philosophies and lies keep me from believing God's Word?
- How did God bring me to a place where I live from and abide in His Word?
- How can I pass my convictions on to the women I meet with?

As you recall how you became convinced of your need for the Scriptures, can you sense how you might help another woman think through her basic need for the Word? If someone is in the early stages of their faith—new to **believing, belonging**, or starting down the road to **becoming**—we must emphasize God's Word in their life.

Here are some topical content ideas as we consider how we might responsibly ground another in His Word. Lessons for these topics can be found in Section One of *The Discipler's Handbook* (see the end of this chapter for more information):

- The Word of God: Inspiration
- The Word of God: Eternal
- The Word of God: Essential
- The Word of God: Powerful
- The Word of God: Obedience
- Daily Life with God in the Word
- The Hand Illustration: Getting a Grasp on God's Word (see the end of this chapter for further explanation)

Here is a brief example of how to lay out this content for a young believer who does not yet have her foundation in the Word:

First, talk with her about the "food" God has given for all believers' growth (1 Peter 2:2).

Second, start with the first topic suggested above: "The Word of God: Inspiration." Carefully guide the time with direction such as, "Let's look at these verses and glean everything we can about the characteristics and benefits of Scripture." This exercise is intended to fully engage not just her mind but also her spirit by letting her share what she sees in the Word. Affirm her as the Spirit gives her insight over the verses.

Third, ask her some personal questions: "Seeing that these things are true about the Scriptures, what should be our response?" "What does it mean for us that Scripture is inspired?" "What encourages you as you realize the value of Scripture?"

Finally, as you progress through these different topics, stress that it is not enough to become intellectually convinced of the value of God's Word. Encourage her to abide daily in His Word.

The best way to teach someone how to have a quiet time is to have one with her. The quiet time is made up of a few components: praying, reading with reflection, and praying again. Start in either the book of Mark or John. Pray before reading a few verses together. Pray that you would hear God's voice as you read His Word together. Then read a group of verses. Reflect on these verses, asking, "What do I learn about Jesus in this passage? Is God saying something specific for me to obey? How does this section of Scripture bless me?"

Reflection on the Word is a skill, and it is a vital part of having a quiet time. Actually having a quiet time with someone we are discipling will be foundational for their future walk with Jesus. When we do this, we are teaching them to feed themselves!

How would you impart the "pure milk" of the Word to someone you are discipling?

Solid Food

Before we engage in thinking about solid-food topics, we must remember that our third category is meat. The main difference between solid-food topics and meat topics is the maturity level and need of the one we are helping.

Solid-food topics are still somewhat basic and very necessary. They can be topics like prayer, the Holy Spirit,

Scripture memory, faith and obedience, Christ as Lord, identity in Christ, sharing Christ through sharing your story, and fellowship. The material in part 1 of this book, concepts crucial for our connection to Christ, falls into this category of food.

The woman you are helping may have studied many of these things in a Bible study group or heard about them at church or a conference. But covering them in one-on-one time provides a strong scriptural basis for each topic and accountability for applying them.

> *When you think of important solid food topics, what comes to your mind?*
> *What topics helped you as a young believer to become rooted and built up in Christ (Colossians 2:6-7)?*

Meat

Most discipling content will flow from the milk and solid food categories above. But we do not want to dismiss our last category: meat. The meat category is for strong disciples who need to have their knowledge and understanding of the Scriptures broadened. The goal as we share meat with another woman is to nurture her depth in the Word and to affirm in her the vision of being used by God to disciple other women. I have found over the years that the list is very dependent on topics the woman I am helping senses she must master or go deeper in. Here are a few examples:

- Advancing and sharing the gospel among the lost around me (relational evangelism versus proclamation evangelism)
- Moral purity
- The tongue
- How to disciple someone
- Character qualities of the believer
- Servanthood
- Overview of the Bible
- The ministry of Jesus Christ
- Understanding the Gospels
- The body of Christ; His church
- Community
- Cultural topics: homosexuality, justice
- Career
- Money
- Relationships: single/married, divorce

What meat topics have rounded out your understanding of Scripture, increased your love for Christ, and strengthened your influence with people around you? How can you help another woman pick up the vision to disciple others?

PREPARING CONTENT

Preparation of content is like putting together a healthy meal for the one we are meeting with. When we have discerned where they are in their process of growth, we are much more able to determine content to share with them.

This responsibility can feel overwhelming if we are not resting in the fact that Jesus is going to help us. As we are involved in discipling others we will grow in our ability to prep and present content. Disciplined effort of prep and the actual presentation of content are how we bring Jesus into the conversation.

Now that we've talked about the categories and the kinds of things we might share, I hope you feel the confidence to think through what topics you might want to go through as you disciple someone. To help in your preparation, go ahead and create a list of potential topics for each category that you can reference later. As an example, here's my list:

MILK	SOLID FOOD	MEAT
1. The New Supernatural Life	1. The Wheel Illustration	1. The Character of God
2. Christ the Center	2. Prayer	2. World Vision
3. The Word of God: Inspiration	3. Identity in Christ	3. Growing in Character
4. The Word of God: Eternal	4. Obedience to Christ	4. Bible Doctrines
5. The Word of God: Essential	5. The Holy Spirit	5. Disciplemaking
6. The Word of God: Powerful	6. Faith	6. Cultural Topics
7. The Word of God: Obedience	7. Your Story or Testimony	7. Deeper Bible Study
8. Daily Life with God in the Word	8. Reaching the Lost	8. And So On!
9. The Hand Illustration	9. Temptation	
10. Who Is a Disciple?	10. The Process Illustration	

NOW IT'S YOUR TURN!

MILK	SOLID FOOD	MEAT

No doubt over the years your list will change a bit. Mine continues to change as I conform to the needs of those I encounter. So don't be annoyed if this happens to you! The purpose of creating a content list is to become skilled at knowing the possibilities and needs for the women we disciple.

Once we have clarity on possible content, then it is time for us to develop some short, simple lessons from Scripture. So you know, for every topic I write at least one lesson that I can share with every woman I might meet with. As I use this lesson with different women, I adapt the presentation of the topic to their personal needs in the given area. Here is a brief outline for prepping content:

CONTENT OUTLINE

I. Select the topic: What is the key thought you want to share?

II. Choose a verse or passage from Scripture that best explains what you sense God wants you to emphasize on this topic.

III. Write a question that segues into the topic naturally and introduces what you hope to find in the verse or passage.

IV. Discuss with reflection questions. Create many questions that will launch you into a reflective discussion.

V. Think of how God used this in your life. Have your story ready!

VI. Apply it. Ask her what she might do in response to what she heard from God on this topic.

Look back to your list of potential topics. Using this content outline, create a simple lesson for two of those topics. There's no need to make it complicated! As you prepare, think through your story—how did you learn about and apply this topic in your life? I always select verses that I know a lot about as the key verses. Here is an example of a basic lesson:

THE WORD OF GOD: ESSENTIAL

I. Key Verses: Matthew 4:1-11; Jeremiah 15:16

II. Key Thought: God gives us His Word so that we might feed upon and draw life from it as one would rely on her daily bread.

III. Key Question: How did Jesus view the Word of God?

IV. Discussion with Reflection Questions:

A. Read Matthew 4:1-11. Where is Jesus in this passage? Where is Satan? What is happening in this scene with Jesus and Satan?

B. What is the first temptation Satan throws at Jesus? How does Jesus counter Satan with this temptation? What does Jesus compare the Word of God to in this interaction? Why do you think He does so?

C. How does Jesus confirm throughout the rest of this scene that God's Word is central for all of the believer's life? What phrase does Jesus repeat in verses 4, 7, and 10? What do we learn by His use of the Word of God?

D. Note that Satan also has the Word of God memorized! What does the craftiness of our enemy, Satan, force us to realize as we seek to know God's Word?

E. Read Jeremiah 15:16. Describe the effects God's Word had on Jeremiah.

F. How does Jeremiah's response to receiving God's Word set an example for us?

V. Discipler Story: Share how God has proven His Word to be essential in your life.

VI. Application: If Jesus quoted the Word of God to overcome temptation, perhaps we need to consider memorizing the Word also. Is the verse we talked about today you might want to memorize?

Creating a simple lesson to share using just a few verses and stories from your own life will no doubt increase your confidence as a disciplemaker. My hope is that by answering the question "What should we share?" removes some of the burden and intimidation you may feel about discipling. When we first begin to disciple women, there is a bit of work to be done so that we can faithfully and responsibly offer content that is in sync with the needs of those we meet with. These skills will serve us well as we disciple others, and eventually our ability to disciple will evolve into an art that easily flows from our personal design.

DISCIPLEMAKER CHALLENGE

- What obstacles or difficulties might you run into in your discipling relationship if you do not do the work of preparation with intentionality?

- Describe how you might communicate your work of preparation with the one you are discipling.

- How do you think the one you are discipling will perceive your preparation and how you share the content?

For specific tools to help a young believer grow, check out *The Discipler's Handbook* at www.thedisciplemaker.org/gentle-art. *The Discipler's Handbook* was created for beginning disciplers as they start to meet with women, offering concrete lesson plans for milk and solid-food topics. These lessons sharply attack the topic and make it simple, short, and applicable. On this web page you will also find the Hand, Wheel, and Process Illustrations, three useful tools that can be used as you disciple someone.

CHAPTER EIGHT

How Does Discipling One-on-One Actually Work?

We work together to serve God. *You are like God's field. You are like his building. God has given me the grace to lay a foundation as a wise builder. Now someone else is building on it.* But each one should build carefully. ⌄ 1 CORINTHIANS 3:9-10, EMPHASIS ADDED

I HAVE ALWAYS ENJOYED EXERCISE—whether it is spinning at home in my basement, taking a brisk, lengthy walk outside, or attending a class at a local gym. Before I suffered from a variety of foot and knee injuries, I attended a local Jazzercise center for seven years. (Jazzercise is basically an hour-long dance-aerobics class with combined emphasis on cardio and strength training.) After attending the class for a while, I realized that there were certain instructors I preferred. I would anticipate the workout I knew they would deliver, and I would do whatever it took to get into those classes!

The best instructors are committed to their clients' success and create workouts that serve the needs of the group. The class is not about them but about what they can offer the participants. The class is enjoyable because it contains variety, new music, and friendship, and the environment is warm and inviting.

My friend Kara is a former owner and instructor of a local Jazzercise franchise. Kara's goal when she prepared for her classes was for each student to walk away from the workout feeling that they had not only worked a variety of muscles but also recognized improvement in their body awareness, strength, and posture. She sought to create flow from one song to the next that maintained intensity while providing clear instruction about what the class was going to do next.

Timing and giving good cues help to build trust in the instructor. A good instructor flexes with people's needs and is prepared to suggest modified movements for those who need them. She will also pay attention to the individuals who make up the group and volunteer helpful hints to those who are moving incorrectly or in unsafe ways.

"Educating the class about their bodies and what they need is vital," Kara told me. "A good instructor does not assume that people know what they are doing. The fitness instructor is to motivate people so that they keep coming back! Motivation is bred by letting the students know that 'this is your hour—Jazz is here for you!'"

I will never forget one day when our center should have

been closed due to snow. But Kara showed up and led a class for two attendees (of which I was one)! Her kindness and love for giving great workouts was infectious and admirable. When I reflect on Kara's workouts, I think, *For Kara, leading a workout has become an art.*

We can learn from the competent enthusiasm of fitness instructors like my friend Kara when we think about the actual one-on-one discipling meeting. Making sincere effort both in planning for time together and implementing every detail proves how much we value those we serve. In this chapter, we examine the details and flow of how a one-on-one meeting actually works as we spend an hour to ninety minutes with someone, seeking to serve them deeply through sharing life, the Word, and prayer. Because we care about those we will disciple, we want to demonstrate that care by wisely organizing our time with them for their good.

BEST PRACTICES FOR DISCIPLING

Let's say someone comes to you and asks you to disciple them, or you have observed someone you would like to invite into a discipling relationship. Now what? We're going to unpack some of what I have learned over the years— what I would call "best practices" for us as we disciple. I had to learn these things, and I learned through failure, mistakes, and success!

The comments and direction you're about to read

are given with the hope that you will develop your own style rather than feel as though you have to copy mine. Remember: discipling is an art, and you are the artist. Every artist takes her tools and learns the basic skills for those tools, but proficiency in skills is not the artist's end goal. The end goal is to be able to paint with expression and beauty, revealing a masterpiece that reflects the Creator's heart. Our Creator has allowed us to engage one-on-one with someone, bringing His truth as our artistic media to the canvas of her life.

Initial Commitment with Clarity

Over my years of both discipling and being discipled, I have always appreciated clarity on what we have committed to in the discipling relationship. When we do not have an initial discussion where we agree upon certain details, we're much more likely to face disappointment, misguided expectations, or confusion, all which lead to the breaking down of a fundamentally important relationship.

When I was in my twenties, I did not pursue this initial discussion with a woman named Danette whom I was going to disciple. I had this covert fear that if we really talked about what we were going to do, she would walk away. Over time, Danette and I became great friends. We met frequently. We hung out and had a lot of fun together.

But eventually the discipling aspect dissipated from our relationship. We were great friends. But the Word and prayer were not established as important between us because we had not clarified what this "discipling" thing was going to look like. I let the focus get away from us. I was inexperienced and fearful, and I regret losing focus. Had I been faithful to the role of gently discipling Danette with clarity, not only would we have certainly become great friends, but there also would have been a fruitful investment from me to her. The question we need to entertain is, "Do you want to end up with just a great friend—or someone who has truly grown in Christ?" Clarifying why and for what we are meeting will ensure both!

Discipling relationships can fizzle out if we do not clarify from the beginning what we are about. To help avert this outcome, we can follow three key steps that help bring clarity:

1. We need to discuss why we are meeting. No matter how sure we are about meeting with someone, we need to discuss and discern whether meeting together is right for both of us. We must not assume that when someone asks, "Will you disciple me?" we both have the same definition for the verb *disciple*, much less the same picture of how that would look.

2. We should invite the person we're meeting with to share what they are looking for. Our questions should be, "So what is it that you are asking for when you talk about discipling?" "What are you hoping for?" "What is your need?" This allows us to discern whether what

we hope to offer is what she is asking for. If what she wants is not what we hope to offer, then the relationship is not a good fit.

3. If we sense that we are on the same page about this discipling relationship, then we both can pray about our commitment to each other. If after sensing God's leading through prayer, we sense that the relationship is still "a go," we can set up a first discipling meeting.

This initial conversation sets the relationship up for a fruitful outcome. When I disciple, I want to know that the woman is serious about the investment we will make together and excited about how God might use this time for her growth. Knowing that she has the qualities we talked about in chapter 6 and that she wants and needs what I hope to offer makes me highly motivated to meet with her.

One caution: Whenever we add a discipling relationship to our lives, we need to make sure that we have adequate space in our schedules to do so. My greatest weakness over the years has been to blurt out yes when someone seems like a great fit for a discipling relationship. But to do this before I look at my schedule is not fair. Let me encourage you to really examine your schedule as you pray about realistically adding this kind of commitment. When we say yes to someone in a new discipling relationship, we want to make sure we are completely present and supportive. We might need to clear a path in our schedule so that we can disciple a hungry heart.

Commitment to Content and Preparation

After the Lord leads both of us to say yes to our discipling relationship, we should discuss what content we might cover as we meet together, as well as the possibility of any assignments or preparation. Normally, we as the disciplers are doing the prep, but sometimes we might assign work that would enhance what we have been talking about. This discussion is important because it covers the intentional aspect of discipling.

Recently I began meeting with a young mom. She has three children ages three and under. As you might imagine, she is in a season of life like none other. So as I thought through content, part of my desire was to reduce any prep she might have. Simplifying our approach helps us get in the Word in a way that best serves her life circumstances.

Keeping Track

I am not the most organized person, but I have learned the importance of keeping track of what takes place in meetings. I keep a folder for each person I am meeting with and bring that folder to our one-on-one time. As we meet, I note what we talk about, the topic we cover, any prayer requests we share, and our next meeting date, if known. If I don't do this, I will forget! This practice gives me the ability to review prior to the next time we meet. I highly encourage keeping track of your time with the woman you're discipling. It may look different from how I do it, but the end goal should be the same.

Practical Questions

After we agree about scriptural content and possible assignments, we can move into some important practical questions:

- What time of day will we meet?
- How often will we meet?
- Where will we meet?
- Over what period of time (six months or a year) will we meet together before evaluating whether to continue our discipling relationship?

These questions lay the needed groundwork for us as we anticipate meeting in the future months. As we answer these questions, we strive to accommodate the needs of the woman we're meeting with. Once we understand what works best for her, we can check our availability to map out a plan that works well for both of us. A mom may wish to meet at her home during her kids' naptime, find a babysitter, or have the children playing nearby. A woman with a full-time job may need to meet during her lunch break or immediately after work. Whatever the situation, our task as disciplers is to set up meeting times with those we help that will best serve them.

The period of time over which we want to meet depends a lot on the frequency of our meetings. If we meet once every week or two weeks, we may want to evaluate whether to continue on in six months. If we are meeting less frequently, then we'll want to evaluate in a year. Understanding the period of time is helpful in making the commitment.

Whenever I have neglected this question (and I have more than I care to admit), our meetings tend to peter out over time. Knowing the practical elements of the discipleship relationship at the outset will help us find success in the long term.

WHAT DOES A MEETING LOOK LIKE?

While we put together some prepared content in the last chapter, prepping content and sharing content are very different. Since my goal is to equip you with practical knowledge and confidence for your discipling relationships, we're going to get very detailed with a suggested plan for the one-on-one meeting. Assuming that we are in a healthy, vibrant discipling relationship, here is a general blueprint for the breakdown of a ninety-minute meeting:

> First thirty to forty minutes: **Catch up on life!** I have also learned to ask during this time, "How are your quiet times going these days?"

> Next thirty to forty minutes: **Time in the Word.** Transitioning into this time begins with the question you wrote in your content outline to naturally segue into the topic. During this time, investigate the Word with the emphasis on how it relates to her life and application.

> Last ten to twenty minutes: **Bring your time together to a close.** You may find that you will interact more deeply

about life issues and worries after your discussion time in the Word. Gather prayer requests that have surfaced from your discussion and from her personal needs for the next week.

Last few minutes: **Pray together.** Sometimes I pray after I find out what my friend would like me to pray about. Sometimes she prays too. All of this depends on what works and is most natural for us. If we meet in a public place like a restaurant or busy coffee shop, then sometimes we forego prayer altogether or go out to the car and pray there.

So that is how we might divide the time of our ninety-minute meeting. Now let's break down the "Time in the Word" piece a little further, beginning with the transition from "Catching Up on Life."

Transition

As we've talked about before, time in the Word during our one-on-one time is a key piece as we disciple. But how do we transition from catching up on life into studying prepared content in the Word? We all know that we could spend hours catching up! And of course we want to sync up our hearts as we catch up, but that is not the only reason we are meeting. If we sense we need more time for "catch up," then that is a great reason to plan separate time together to develop the relationship. Transitioning to time in the Word may feel awkward, but really it can be as simple as saying something like, "Wow, so much is happening in both our lives! Today we are going to really dig into the heart of Jesus and see how He viewed the Word of God, okay?"

The Topic

After we have transitioned into our time in the Word, we need to state the key question. Then, we can open the Scriptures and have the one we're meeting with read the key verses for the topic. If necessary, we can restate the key question in different words: "As you read these verses out loud, let's both look for statements Jesus made that reveal how He viewed the Word." After she reads, we can step into Discussion with Reflection.

Discussion with Reflection

The purpose of discussion with reflection is to ponder His Word together. The skills of discipling that we use during this time and continue to develop are (1) learning to prepare and ask discriminating questions and (2) being personally involved with the Scriptures ourselves so we can pass the Word on.

How we personally contemplate the Word in our walk with Jesus will definitely impact our ability to lead this time of discussion. Leading a discussion with reflection is where the "gentle art" of discipling is front and center. It is an art to discern which questions will not only lead her to go deep in the Word but help her reflect on what the Spirit is saying to her.

We want to invite her to go deeper into the Word by asking good questions, but ultimately we want the Holy Spirit to speak into her growth. Sometimes she will have an "aha" moment, but most of the time we will see a qualitative increase of her understanding of Christ and His ways. This discussion over the Word will over time bear fruit toward maturity.

During our time of reflection over the Word, we should strive to let the one we are discipling do the talking. I find it helpful to spend time on my own in the passage or verse beforehand so that I am personally connected to it. One of the greatest blessings of discipling another is the opportunity to reread familiar passages and discover new facets of understanding for our lives. Invariably, the one we disciple will open up new thoughts as we ponder together. As disciplers, we might close our time of discussion with our "prepared story" to give our personal example of how we apply the verses. Again, let God lead in the midst of the time together.

Application

During the application segment we want to pull together the various threads that were uncovered from the verse or passage to help the woman we're discipling see where she is in relationship to the topic. We may ask questions like, "So how does knowing Jesus' perspective of the scriptures influence you today?" or "As we were reading through this passage about Jesus, did you sense the Holy Spirit speaking into your life?"

In the application time, we want to discern what action we will take as a result of our understanding from Scripture. As we search out possible applications, the one we are helping will likely connect these thoughts with other areas of application in her life. This is good and healthy. It is her walk with Christ that is in process, and we can serve her by bringing accountability to her desired application.

The actual one-on-one meeting should deepen your relationship with each other, but more importantly it should deepen her attachment to Jesus. The outcomes from these one-on-one meetings are subjective and will develop over time. As disciplers, we must continue to follow God's leading and be faithful as we intentionally and relevantly present content to those we are helping.

WHEN TO GO OFF PLAN

Now even though it is vital to plan and be prepared, we also need to understand that individual meetings or even discipling relationships will not necessarily go the way we're planning. We need to also be prepared to respond to a one-on-one meeting that goes "off plan."

First, we must remain alert to the person's needs and be flexible enough to address those needs. Recently I was meeting with a young woman who was feeling very drained and upset with several relationships with coworkers. I sensed that our planned topic was not going to "make sense" as she shared her life situation, and so wrote "next time" in my folder with her name on it. We then proceeded to discuss and pray over some ideas that might help her handle some "work stress" in the next few days. We were able to look at her situation from God's perspective. I worked at asking her questions that would help her unwrap what was really bothering her. My goal was not to solve her problem but to open a few doors of understanding from her insights. A couple of Scripture verses came to mind, and we mapped out some possible action steps she could take. We prayed together over this, and our time together was good. If you face something like this in a discipling meeting, I encourage you to see the situation not as "off topic" but as "real life" discipleship that trumps your plan. You can pick up your prepared plan at the next meeting.

Second, we may face a situation in which the overall discipling relationship isn't working out in a way that's helpful for the woman involved. This is when we face a key question: Is there a time to end the discipling relationship? The answer is yes.

You might consider "letting someone go" if:

1. She is regularly late, or consistently does not show up.

2. She does not seem to be connecting the dots of God's action in her life or taking application seriously.

3. She regularly dominates the time and leads away from the topic to what she wants to discuss.

4. You begin to feel something is "off" or continually feel frustration as you disciple her. Be in prayer, seek counsel, and let God lead you! The Holy Spirit plays an important role in our discernment process.

I once met with a fairly "mature" believer named Darla. Darla and I had agreed on our purpose for meeting, but as we regularly engaged in meeting one-on-one Darla would take control and direct our conversation toward unhealthy discussions of people (gossip). This happened repeatedly. I was feeling frustrated. I gently but firmly confronted her with how we were wasting our time off topic and not utilizing our time for her growth as we had originally decided upon. She agreed. But after several more meetings, her habit of controlling the conversation continued.

During these weeks I was praying about her continual detour from what we had agreed upon. He revealed to me that rather than receiving the help we had agreed upon, Darla was dominating the time and using my listening ear for her own ends. So God led me to "let her go." It was very difficult for me, but I needed to follow His leading that "enough was enough."

If we let someone go in a discipling relationship, we need to share why. First, we must affirm that we will remain friends, and then we should explain that our agreed-upon purposes are not being met. With Darla, we remained friends, and over time I saw God work in this area of her life through other relationships and in many different ways.

We cannot make someone grow or change, but we can make every effort to serve them. And sometimes this means being flexible in the midst of our one-on-one—or even "letting them go."

THE WOMAN WHO DID WHAT SHE COULD

Throughout this book I have worked at sharing the optimal blueprint for discipling another woman. Now it is up to you to move from the ideal discipling methods to the reality of your life situation as you apply getting involved as a discipler. Intentionally planning and implementing our meetings are important—but more important as we seek to disciple another is that we submit our hearts to Christ and simply do what we can to serve Him. This is the ultimate foundation of our time spent discipling.

During our family's time in Indonesia, my role in ministry felt a bit constrained. My days were filled with raising three elementary-age children in a foreign culture. Everything in life went slowly. I constantly struggled with having enough water for our family to shower in and to boil for drinking. We had helpers who were adept at "mowing" the lawn with a machete-like lawn knife and doing our laundry using a Maytag wringer washer. Our "dryer" was a convenient structure that allowed us to hang many clothes in the sun. Our helper, Ibu Icah, ironed every piece of clothing, even underwear, so that it would be completely dry and neat! I had no need for the Hoover vacuum cleaner I had laboriously shipped to our new home, as the floors were made of concrete-like tile and swept daily using brooms made from coconut hair. Life was different. We adjusted, but the time and energy I had left over after daily responsibilities seemed minimal.

I felt so torn whenever I would think about our purposes for coming to Indonesia. I wanted to be involved in our ministry to students like my husband was, not just overseeing the daily needs of our household. Of course, I was happy to be a mom and loved the opportunities I had to engage at the kids' school. But I still desired to disciple women. I felt isolated and deeply wanted to make a contribution.

As I journeyed through this season of personal desperation, God sent a visiting missionary named Nate to our home. One morning, Nate asked Tom and me if we could open the Word together and see what God might have for us. I had shared with Nate the "ministry melancholy" I was experiencing, so he chose this passage from Mark:

> The Passover and the Feast of Unleavened Bread were only two days away. The chief priests and the teachers of the law were plotting to arrest Jesus secretly. They wanted to kill him. "But not during the feast," they said. "The people may stir up trouble."
>
> Jesus was in Bethany. He was at the table in the home of Simon, who had a skin disease. A woman came with a special sealed jar. It contained very expensive perfume made out of pure nard. She broke the jar open and poured the perfume on Jesus' head.

Some of the people there became angry. They said to one another, "Why waste this perfume? It could have been sold for more than a year's pay. The money could have been given to poor people." So they found fault with the woman.

"Leave her alone," Jesus said. "Why are you bothering her? She has done a beautiful thing to me. You will always have poor people with you. You can help them any time you want to. But you will not always have me. *She did what she could.* She poured perfume on my body to prepare me to be buried. What I'm about to tell you is true. What she has done will be told anywhere the good news is preached all over the world. It will be told in memory of her."

MARK 14:1-9, EMPHASIS ADDED

As the three of us ruminated on the life of this woman who truly loved Jesus and wielded all she had to worship Him, I heard Christ speak to me. I identified with her so completely—she did what she could with what she had to worship Jesus, even while she was reviled by those around her. When Jesus defended her and said, "She did what she could," it was as if He was telling me how I might step forward in ministry in the years ahead. I began to focus on two questions: "What do I have?" and "What can I do?"

This passage helped me to accept my circumstances and reconcile them with my desire for involvement. I experienced a growing peace as I went forward in this season of my life. "She did what she could" became the prayer sieve for all my future decisions and efforts in ministry. And Mark 14:8 has become a staying "power verse" that has underscored most ministry decisions since.

As I mentioned in chapter 6, it was during this phase of my life that I learned to rely on Tom, who was directing the student ministry, and our friend and staff woman Butet for help connecting in ministry. I just felt so powerless in that I could not give what I had hoped. I explained my sense of inadequacy to them. We prayed over what I "could" do. Eventually Tom and Butet asked me to help a few amazing young women through meeting with them one-on-one. Meeting with one or two students was all I could do. And so I did what I could. The pangs of guilt and anxiety I had been experiencing in my "ministry melancholy" began to dissipate as I worshiped Jesus by doing what I could.

I love that this woman in Mark 14, despite the seething atmosphere of hate and murder that surrounded the feast, decided to come and worship Jesus in the only way she knew how. She brazenly but quietly entered into the home of Simon, who had a skin disease. And there were no medical treatments for skin issues like we have today! She risked her personal safety and reputation as well as her health when she carried in the highly valued perfume to anoint the One who was about to give His life for her. She saw Jesus for who He truly was. She didn't agree with those who wanted to kill Him or with those who felt she had wasted her valuable perfume. She understood that she was limited in that she could only do this one thing to connect with the One who was saving her soul. So she did what she could!

📖 GO DEEPER

As we observe and consider the woman in Mark 14, let's examine her life circumstances, her desire to worship Jesus, Jesus' response to her, and the impact of her choices as she "did what she could." Read the passage from Mark 14:1-9 in your favorite translation, and prayerfully answer the questions below in your journal.

Verses 1-2

1. What were the current realities surrounding this visit to Bethany?
2. How might these realities have affected the decision and determination of the woman who came to anoint Jesus?

Verse 3

3. Why did the woman come to see Jesus?
4. What does her selection of "pure nard" tell us about her heart and motivation?

Verses 4-5

5. What was the reaction of some of the people at this dinner regarding her choice to worship Jesus in this way?
6. Why did they see her action as waste rather than worship?
7. Why do you think they were so quick to find fault with her?

8. How do you think the woman felt at that moment?

Verses 6-7

9. How did Jesus respond to those finding fault with the woman and her actions?

10. Jesus described her actions as a "beautiful thing." How do you think she felt when He not only defended her but described what she did as good and beautiful?

Verse 8

11. What did Jesus say that helps us to more deeply understand this woman's comprehension of who He was and her personal desire to worship Him?

12. What did Jesus mean when He said, "She did what she could"?

Verse 9

13. What was the impact of her actions?

14. Do you think she planned this impact? Why or why not?

15. How do you think she felt when Jesus said this about what she had done?

16. As you ponder over this passage, what comes to your mind as you think about the choice to get involved with discipling women?

17. What hindrances do you anticipate?

18. How do the words *She did what she could* describe your life? What strengths do you bring as you contemplate discipling someone?

FINDING STRENGTH

The strength of the woman in Mark 14, as I see it, is that she knew what she wanted to do—worship Jesus. She knew what she had to work with—a worshipful heart and some very expensive perfume. She probably could sense a certain level of hostility as she entered into the courtyard where dinner would be served. But knowing what she did have, a grateful heart and pint of nard, enabled her to go and do what she wanted to do: worship Jesus. She did not let the things she didn't have inhibit her from worshiping. And most importantly, she had the support of Jesus. When we disciple women by doing what we can, we know that Jesus will stand with us.

As we engage in Christ's call to make disciples, we must not get distracted by what we cannot do or those things that might inhibit us. Rather, let us step out in faith and do what we can!

- Identify what you do not have. What prohibits you from stepping forward and by faith discipling one other woman? Are you able to release these hindrances to Jesus?

- Identify what you do have. What enables you to step forward and by faith disciple others? Are you able to offer these abilities as worship unto Jesus?

- If you were to imagine that Jesus was standing next to you right now, what would you say to Him about what you do have and what you don't have when it comes to discipling? What do you think He would say to you?

Lord Jesus, each of us has strengths and weaknesses.
Each of us aspires to the wonderful mission of discipling

others. With this prayer we submit all that we are, all that we have, and all we can do. We ask that You would give our efforts eternal impact for Your glory.

GO OUT

Discipling women is a great and lofty pursuit driven by hearts that want to obey Christ's call. As we prayerfully step forward to disciple someone, we must launch from who we are in Christ. Our personal walk with God, deeply rooted in humbly loving and obeying Him, is our foundation.

My prayer is that this book equips and encourages you for this amazing journey into discipling another woman. We started with four foundational realities that are essential to the caliber of our faith as authentic followers of Christ. We did this because the depth of our walk with Christ will affect the breadth of our ability to disciple another. The in-depth, practical part of discipling that we covered in the second half of this book is shared with the hope that you will have a skillful foundation as you grow into the gentle art of discipling another.

Jesus' very last words to the remaining eleven disciples were not a suggestion but a command: "Go and make disciples." This command certainly is full of challenge. We cannot achieve it apart from the supernatural presence, care, and intervention of the living God. As you respond to our Savior's command in joyful obedience, remember: you are not alone. This gentle art of discipling women is His idea, and as we make the effort, He will bring it to pass! (See 1 Thessalonians 5:24.)

DISCIPLEMAKER CHALLENGE

- Who will you disciple?

- When will you get started?

- Pray over Jeremiah 33:3, and ask God to do great and mighty things in and through you as you disciple others.

Leader's Guide

THIS LEADER'S GUIDE IS DESIGNED to equip you and prepare you for your time leading a small group of women through the material in this book. Remember that these are only suggestions—each group will have its own dynamics and needs, and you'll want to be sensitive to those.

GETTING STARTED

1. Take time to read the book and do the included Bible studies. Sit before the Lord and talk with Him about your personal desire to live authentically and obediently unto Jesus. Begin asking Him how you might take part in what He is doing in the lives of women around you.

2. Pray over who you might invite to the group. Start a list. Consider women around you whom you know,

care about, and want to share with in a vulnerable way. Let people know that you are thinking about doing this study and why. Talk with people who might benefit or know others who might benefit: friends, women at church, your pastor or women's director, etc.

Invite the women who are interested to seriously contemplate their walk with God. Do they sense that their walk is real and honest, or do they feel they have hidden anxieties and fears? Are they engaging personally in the challenges of reaching the lost and discipling?

3. Ask God to show you who to invite. Invite six to eight women to join you. This group size allows for great discussion, good relationships, and depth in sharing.

4. Clarify the commitment you are inviting your group to make. Interact with them, decide together, and then let them know the day and time of meeting, frequency of gathering, and period of time required. Meeting in a home would be best. Taking turns at different homes or personally hosting creates opportunities to get to know one another better.

THE ENVIRONMENT FOR THE STUDY

Invite the women in your group to open, vulnerable, confidential sharing. When others know what we struggle with and care about us, we have support. Together we can entrust the things to Christ that we are tempted to hide. As leader of the group, model vulnerability and create a safe environment in the group. Make sure each group member agrees that what is shared and prayed over will be held in confidence.

Invite the group to think through ideas that will improve the quality of your gatherings, such as turning off cell phones, starting and ending on time, allowing everyone in the group to share, and holding each other accountable for dominating the discussion. In one group I led, we agreed that we would not bring up politics!

As the group leader, you must come prepared, having thought through the schedule. At the beginning of each meeting, let the group know what you hope to accomplish during the time. This sets everyone up for cohesiveness and helps you to steer the conversation back on course when need be. In order to pull everyone back together, don't be afraid to kindly and firmly point out that the group is getting off topic.

MATERIALS

Each person will need a copy of the book, a discipleship notebook, and their Bible. The discipleship notebook can be used to log thoughts and answers to the scriptural studies, keep notes, and track personal applications.

COMMITMENT TO THE STUDY

To join this study, women should agree to carefully read and thoughtfully answer the chapter questions for each meeting. They should also be willing to share honestly as they are led.

COMPLETING THE BOOK

As the group leader, you must decide how your group will complete this book. Here are two possible scenarios:

Scenario One: Since the book is divided into two sections, take some time to go through the introduction before you enter a particular part of the book. Then within that section, take two weeks per chapter. The first week, pursue an overview of the entire chapter. The second week, delve into the scriptural study.

Deciding to meet twice per chapter allows you to build a relational component into your gathering times. I suggest that during a two-hour study time you spend twenty to thirty minutes catching up as a group, as well as time praying together and sharing life stories. You may also wish to allow the group to answer a question that will bring them closer together. For example: "Who in my life offered me love or acceptance that helped me to understand God's love for me more clearly?"

When the group completes part 1 of the book, use a meeting time for fun, games, brunch, or something else the whole group would enjoy before moving into part 2. In all the groups I have led, there seems to be at least one or two women who are just waiting to organize an enjoyable time like this—so I let them!

Scenario Two: Cover the whole book in one semester (fall or spring). Each week, cover one chapter. If you have more than eight weeks, use the extra weeks for relationship building (share life stories, have a brunch, play games, etc.)!

ENCOURAGING ACTION

Part 2 leads the participants into the practical aspects of discipling women. As you lead this section, discuss questions openly, encouraging the women to share their doubts, fears, and hindrances, all the while reminding the group of the importance of trusting Christ by faith when they step out to disciple another woman. Women may feel intimidated by discussing who they might disciple, but doing so will encourage and inspire the group to move forward. As members of your group begin to step out and disciple someone else, create opportunities for the group to gather together and discuss how it is going. No one needs to be the expert; everyone needs to be a learner!

Notes

1. *Merriam-Webster's Collegiate Dictionary*, s.v. "discipleship."
2. God uses several means to establish believers in their faith: corporate worship, small groups, and one-on-one discipling. In this book, we will concentrate on the one-on-one relationship in discipling. To achieve healthy spiritual growth, every young Christian should be related to a small group as well as a larger body of believers like the local church or Christian groups on campus. While critical, one-on-one relationship alone can result in a narrow and lopsided kind of growth (Tom Yeakley, "The Nuts and Bolts of One-to-One Discipling," 1997, http://www.goprojectimpact.com/resources/documents/The%20Nuts%20and%20Bolts%20of%20One%20to%20One%20Discipling.pdf).
3. Spiros Zodhiates, ed., *The Hebrew-Greek Key Word Study Bible* (Chattanooga, TN: AMG, 2008), 1838.
4. Frederica Mathewes-Green, *At the Corner of East and Now* (Chesterton, IN: Conciliar Press, 2008), 32.
5. Used with permission. Name has been changed to protect privacy.
6. C. S. Lewis, *Perelandra* (New York: Scribner, 1996), 186.
7. C. S. Lewis, *The Weight of Glory* (New York: HarperCollins, 2001), 182.
8. Robert Loveless, "Every Day with Jesus," 1936.
9. F. B. Meyer, *The Secret of Guidance* (Chicago: Moody, 2010).
10. *Strong's Exhaustive Concordance of the Bible*, Updated and Expanded Edition (Peabody, MA: Hendrickson Publishers, 2007), 2315.
11. Watchman Nee, *The Normal Christian Life* (Carol Stream, IL: Tyndale, 1977), 179–180.
12. Walter Liefeld, "Luke," *Zondervan NIV Bible Commentary*, edited by Kenneth Barket and John Kohlenberger III (Grand Rapids: Zondervan, 1994).

13. Jill Briscoe, *The One Year Devotions for Women* (Carol Stream, IL: Tyndale, 2000), 327.

14. Zodhiates, ed., *The Hebrew-Greek Key Word Study Bible*, 1853.

15. Amy Carmichael, *If* (Fort Washington, PA: CLC Publications, 2011), 47.

16. Amy Martin, women's director at Harvest Bible Chapel in Naperville, Illinois. Used with permission.

17. Linnette Bachman, "Feminine Disciplemaking" (self-published pamphlet).

18. Carmichael, *If*, 17.

19. Elisabeth Elliot, *Let Me Be a Woman* (Carol Stream, IL: Tyndale, 1976), 171.

Woman's Journey of Discipleship series

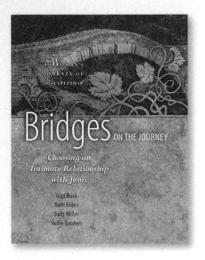

Woman's Journey of Discipleship series is written by women for women, and it helps them to establish their faith, grow into Christ's likeness, and share their faith. The *Bridges on the Journey* study is the first book in the series. Freshly revised, this study is designed for women who are just beginning their journey with Christ and are learning to develop lifelong habits that will transform their lives and impact the lives of others.

Bridges on the Journey
Book 1 of Woman's Journey of Discipleship series
978-1-60006-786-0 | 6 Weeks | $12.99

Other books in the series include

Crossroads on the Journey
Book 2 of Woman's Journey of Discipleship

For women who want to grow deeper in their relationship with Christ and learn to make decisions based on scriptural principles for life transformation.

978-1-60006-785-3
8 weeks | $12.99

Friends on the Journey
Book 3 of Woman's Journey of Discipleship

For women who are established in their faith and seek to disciple other women.

978-1-63146-538-3
8 weeks | $12.99

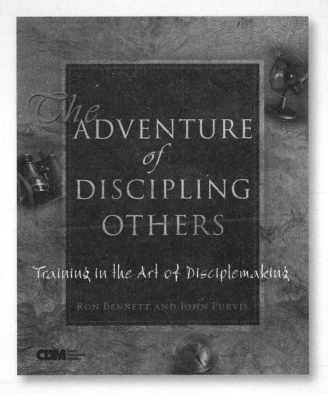